Fodor's POCKET first edition

# nantucket

fodor's travel publications
new york • toronto • london • sydney • auckland
www.fodors.com

# contents

## maps

# ON THE ROAD WITH FODOR'S

**EVERY VACATION IS IMPORTANT.** So here at Fodor's we've pulled out all stops in preparing *Pocket Nantucket*. To direct you to the places that are truly worth your time and money, we've rallied the team of endearingly picky know-it-alls we're pleased to call our writers. If you knew them, you'd poll them for tips yourself.

**Elizabeth Gehrman** has seen the sights of Europe, Hong Kong, the Caribbean, South Africa, Canada, and thirty of the fifty states. She is managing editor of *Boston College Magazine*, and has written travel stories and features for several newspapers and Web sites, including the *Boston Herald*, the *New York Times*, and harvard.net.news.

**Lynda Hammes** is cross-country (and concrete) runner and an assistant editor at *Art & Auction*—two skills which made her a valuable contributor to the Outdoor Activities and Sports chapter.

**Sandy MacDonald** is a truly accomplished and prolific travel writer having contributed to many Nantucket, Boston, and New England travel guides. She has also written on Nantucket for several newspapers and magazines including *Boston Magazine*, *Boston Globe*, *Country Home*, *Country Inns*, and the *Nantucket Inquirer & Mirror*.

**Bill Maple,** Director of Natural Sciences at Nantucket's Maria Mitchell Association, and a professor of biology at Bard College, wrote the wildlife boxes and glossaries in the Outdoor Activities and Sports chapter.

**Debi Stetson** has written on Cape Cod, Martha's Vineyard, and Nantucket for travel guides and *The Cape Codder*, *Antiques & Arts*, *Cape Cod Home*, and *Cape Cod Life* among others.

**Joyce Wagner** is a freelance travel writer whose credits include *Cape Cod Life*, *Cape Cod Home & Garden*, and the *Martha's Vineyard Times*. She is also a published short story writer.

## Don't Forget to Write

Keeping a travel guide fresh and up-to-date is a big job. So we love your feedback—positive and negative—and follow up on all suggestions. Contact the *Pocket Nantucket* editor at editors@fodors.com or c/o Fodor's, 280 Park Avenue, New York, New York 10017. And have a wonderful trip!

Karen Cure
Editorial Director

# nantucket

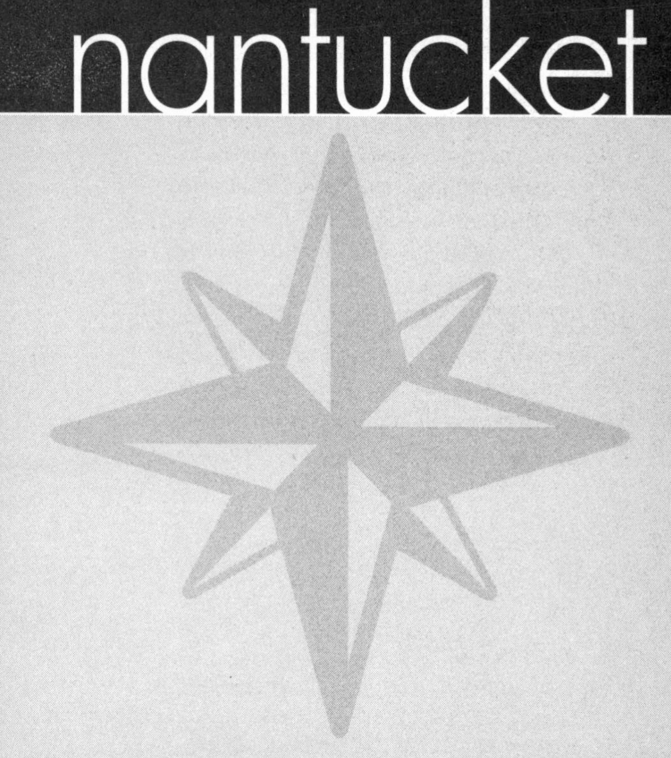

*In some ways mogul Ronald Perelman's mega-yacht—super-sized at 300 feet—has come to symbolize the paradoxical success of Nantucket tourism. Seeking a simple-living retreat from the urban rat race, an increasingly sophisticated pool of repeat visitors brought equally high-caliber accoutrements to the island: superlative restaurants, sumptuously appointed B&Bs, chic clothing boutiques and antiques shops, and, of course, private yachts. Remembering Nantucket's working-class whaling-industry roots, it is amusing to imagine what the captains of yore would have made of Perelman's massive vessel, having themselves plied the waters of the world in fast, fleet clipper ships a fraction of its size.*

## In This Chapter



By Sandy MacDonald

# introducing nantucket

**FOR THE FIRST TIME** since its golden age as a world-renowned whaling capital in the early 1800s, the tiny island of Nantucket is decidedly on a roll. Modest shingled cottages that might have gone begging for a buyer a decade ago now fetch an easy million. The 800-plus pre-1840 structures that compose the core of town—a National Landmark Historic District—only rarely change hands, and then at exalted prices. As for the trophy houses—mega-mansions built in the hinterlands for rich arrivistes—they're constantly off the charts, setting new records only to break them.

And yet its ascending chic has very little to do with what attracts most people to Nantucket in the first place, or keeps them coming back. The allure has more to do with how, at the height of summer, a cooling fog will drift in across the multihued moors or the way rambling wild roses, the gaudy pink Rosa rugosa, perfume a hidden path to the beach.

Essentially Nantucket is *all* beach—a boomerang-shape sandspit consisting of detritus left by a glacier that receded millennia ago. Off Cape Cod, some 26 mi out to sea, the island measures 3½ by 14 mi at its widest points, while encompassing—such are the miracles of inlet and bay—more than 100 mi of sandy shoreline, all of it open, as a matter of local pride, to absolutely everyone.

Whereas elsewhere along the New England coast private interests have carved prime beachfront into exclusive enclaves,

Nantucketers are resolved that the beaches should remain accessible to the general public. A half-dozen or so town-supervised beaches have amenities such as snack bars and lifeguard stations. The rest are the purview of solitary strollers—or, unfortunately, ever-growing convoys of dune-destroying SUVs. Nantucket's laissez-faire approach to beach management poses a delicate and perhaps ultimately untenable balancing act. So far islanders seem shockingly sanguine about the escalating presence of cars on their pristine beaches, even as they carp about congestion in town.

This is but one of the issues that percolate to the surface every April, during a weeklong Town Meeting that draws a good portion of the island's 6,000 year-round residents (the summer population can expand to eight times that figure). Far more immediate are concerns about overbuilding. Even with 40% of the island in some form of conservation trust, sprawl is a pressing issue: although there's a cap, maximum buildup is projected within the next few decades. And as real-estate prices soar, middle-class options shrink. The island is currently in the throes of "Aspenization," wherein the working families who support the largely service-based economy are rapidly being priced out. Only here, the dispossessed can't just move to a nearby town.

The level of concern is such that, in 2000, Nantucket made the National Trust for Historic Preservation's list of Most Endangered Historic Places, a dubious honor at best. At present the island is too prosperous for its own good—a paradise in crisis. But residents are actively addressing these and other concerns and are building consensus for a Comprehensive Plan that will include affordable housing and sustainable businesses.

Still, on a day when sun scintillates on sand and the thrumming waves hint at an eternal rhythm, it's hard to imagine that anything could ever go too terribly wrong here. As summer succeeds summer, children will continue to construct their fanciful if foredoomed sand castles and marvel over the odd treasures the tides drag in. Adults will gladly play along, if allowed, remembering their own seemingly endless days of summer and imagining more of the same for their children's children and so on and on. Perfection can be surprisingly simple, after all, and even if Nantucket's current cachet should fade, the island's timeless pleasures will endure.

## THE MAKING OF NANTUCKET

At the height of its prosperity in the early to mid-19th century, this tiny island was the world's foremost whaling port. Its harbor bustled with the coming and going of whaling ships and coastal merchant vessels putting in for trade or outfitting. Along the wharves a profusion of sail lofts, ropewalks, ship's chandleries, cooperages, and other shops stood cheek by jowl. Barrels of whale oil were off-loaded from ships onto wagons, then wheeled along cobblestone streets to refineries and candle factories. On strong sea breezes the smoke and smells of booming industry were carried through the town as inhabitants eagerly took care of business. It's no wonder that Herman Melville's Ishmael, of the novel *Moby-Dick*, felt the way he did about the place:

*My mind was made up to sail in no other than a Nantucket craft, because there was a fine, boisterous something about everything connected with that famous old island, which amazingly pleased me.*

But the island's boom years didn't last long. Kerosene came to replace whale oil, sought-after sperm whales were overhunted and became scarce, and a sandbar at the mouth of the harbor silted up. Before the prosperity ended, however, enough hard-won profits went into building the grand houses that remind us of the glory days. And wharves once again teem with shops that tend to the needs of incoming ships—ferry boats, mostly, and luxury yachts, whose passengers crave elegant accoutrements in lieu of ropes and barrels.

Thanks in no small part to the island's isolation in the open Atlantic—its original Native American name, Nanticut, means

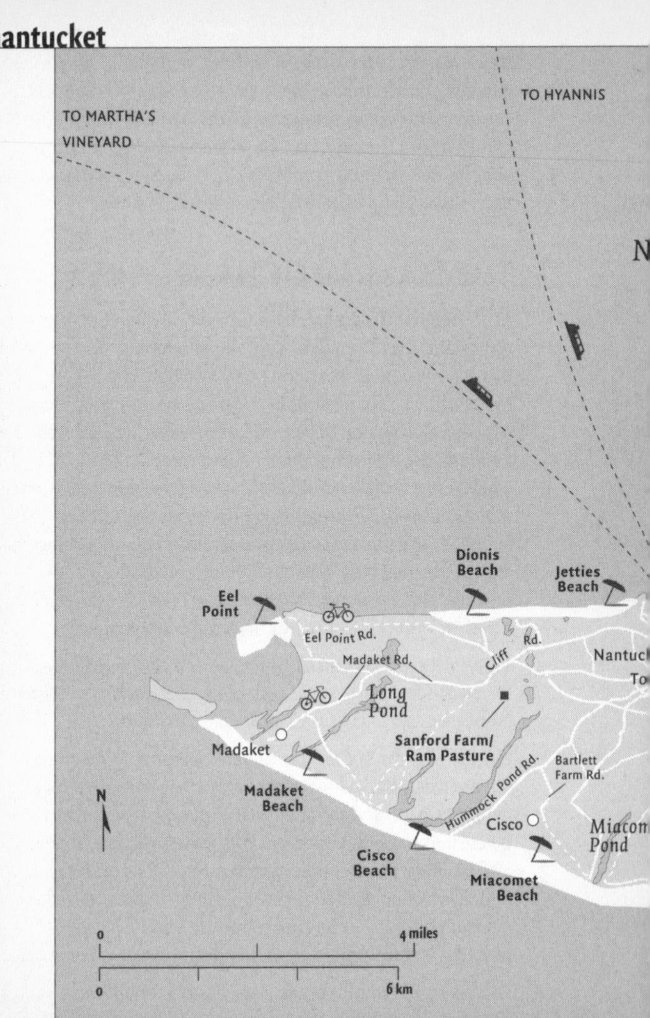
TO MARTHA'S VINEYARD
TO HYANNIS
Dionis Beach
Jetties Beach
Eel Point
Eel Point Rd.
Rd.
Cliff
Madaket Rd.
Nantuc
To
Long Pond
Madaket
Sanford Farm/ Ram Pasture
Madaket Beach
Hummock Pond Rd.
Bartlett Farm Rd.
N
Cisco
Miacom Pond
Cisco Beach
Miacomet Beach
0
4 miles
0
6 km

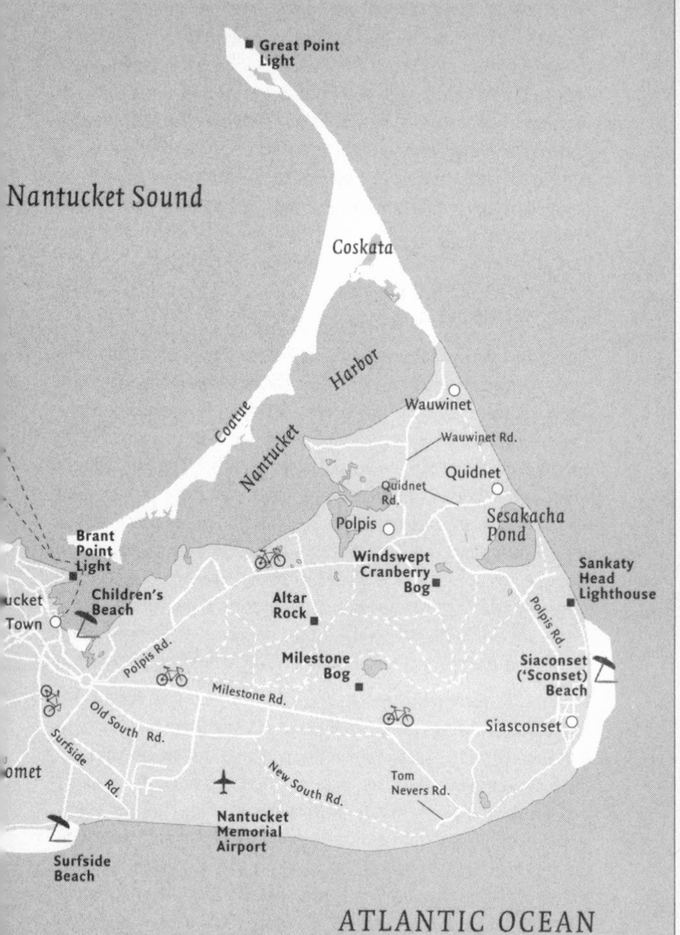
Great Point Light
Nantucket Sound
Coskata
Harbor
Coatue
Nantucket
Wauwinet
Wauwinet Rd.
Quidnet
Quidnet Rd.
Polpis
Sesakacha Pond
Brant Point Light
Windswept Cranberry Bog
Sankaty Head Lighthouse
ucket Town
Children's Beach
Altar Rock
Polpis Rd.
Polpis Rd.
Milestone Bog
Siaconset ('Sconset) Beach
Milestone Rd.
Old South Rd.
Surfside Rd.
Siasconset
omet
New South Rd.
Tom Nevers Rd.
Nantucket Memorial Airport
Surfside Beach
ATLANTIC OCEAN

"faraway land"—and to an economy that experienced frequent depressions, Nantucket has managed to retain much of its 17th- to 19th-century character. The town itself hardly seems to have changed since whaling days: streets are still lined with hundreds of historic houses and lit by old-fashioned lamps. This remarkable preservation also owes much to the foresight and diligence of people working to ensure that Nantucket's uniqueness can be enjoyed by generations to come. In 1955 legislation was initiated to designate Nantucket Town an official National Historic District. Now any outwardly visible alterations to a structure, even the installation of air conditioners or a change in the color of paint, must conform to a rigid building code.

The code's success shows in the harmony of the buildings, most covered in weathered gray shingles, sometimes with a clapboard facade painted white or gray. With local wood in short supply, clapboard facades were a sign of wealth. In town, which is more strictly regulated than the outskirts, virtually nothing jars. Island-wide, you'll find no neon, stoplights, billboards, or fast-food franchises. In spring and summer, when the many tidy gardens are in bloom and cascades of roses cover the gray shingles, the scene seems poised for a postcard. Although the current landscape would be all but unrecognizable to denizens of centuries past—when sheep outnumbered human occupants—key historic landmarks are still ensconced in a setting respectful of the past.

The first Europeans came to the island to escape repressive religious authorities on the mainland. Having themselves fled to the New World to escape persecution in England, the Puritans of the Massachusetts Bay Colony proceeded to persecute Quakers and those who were friendly with them. In 1659 Thomas Macy, who had obtained Nantucket through royal grant and a deal with the resident Wampanoag tribe, sold most of the island to nine shareholders for £30 and two beaver-skin hats. These "original purchasers" then sold half-shares to artisans whose skills the new settlement would need. The names of these early families—Macy, Coffin, Starbuck, Coleman, Swain, Gardner, Folger, and others—appear at every turn in Nantucket, where their many descendants continue to reside.

The first year, Thomas Macy and his family, along with Edward Starbuck and the 12-year-old Isaac Coleman, spent fall and winter at Madaket, getting by with the assistance of local Wampanoags. The following year, 1660, Tristram Coffin and others arrived, establishing a community—later named Sherburne—at Capaum Harbor on the north shore. When storms closed the harbor early in the 18th century, the center of activity was moved to the present Nantucket Town. Relations with the Wampanoags remained cordial; however, the native population—numbering about 3,000 when the settlers arrived—was decimated by plague in 1763. The last full-blooded Wampanoag on the island died in 1855.

Initially the settlers subsisted by farming (crops, they found, did poorly in the sandy soil), raising sheep (free of predators, the island lent itself well to this pursuit), and catching abundant cod. The native Wampanoags also showed them how to spear 50-ton right whales—so-called because they float once killed and can be towed toward land—right from shore. In 1690 the Nantucketers sent for a Cape Cod whaler to teach them to catch whales from small boats just offshore; soon the island's entire south shore was given over to this industry. In 1712 one of the boats happened to be blown farther out to sea and managed to capture a sperm whale, whose spermaceti was much more highly prized than oil. Thus began the whaling era on Nantucket.

In the 18th century, whaling voyages never lasted much longer than a year. By the 19th century the usual whaling grounds had been so depleted that ships had to travel to the Pacific to find their quarry, so trips could last years. Some Nantucket captains actually have South Sea islands named for them—Swain's Reef, Gardner Pinnacles, and so forth. The life of a whaler was very hard, and many never made it home. An account by Owen Chase, first mate of the Nantucket whaling ship *Essex*, of "the mysterious and mortal attack" of a sperm whale, which in 1820 ended in the loss of the ship and most of the crew, fascinated a young sailor named Herman Melville and formed the basis of his 1851 novel, *Moby-Dick*. Recently, that story once again captured the public imagination in the form of the best-selling *In the Heart of the Sea: The Tragedy of the Whaleship Essex* by local historian Nathaniel Philbrick.

The fortunes of Nantucket's whaling industry rose and fell with the tides of three wars and the devastating Great Fire of 1846, which destroyed the port and a good part of town. Just as the islanders struggled to recover (many residents decamped to try to find their fortunes in the California gold rush), the market for whale oil was eclipsed by the introduction of petroleum-based kerosene. By 1861, at the outset of the Civil War—Nantucket had proved its abolitionist mettle early on by outlawing slavery in 1770—the population had plummeted from 10,000 to 2,000.

The hard-strapped stragglers were only too happy to take in boarders, which worked out well with the growth of a postwar leisure class. Toward the end of the century the town supported no fewer than 50 guest houses; a narrow-gauge railroad carried curious tourists out to stroll the quaint town of 'Sconset, whose rose-covered fishing shacks attracted a colony of summering Broadway actors. A vestige of those golden days survives as the Siasconset Casino, a magnificent 1899 Shingle-style theater where 'Sconset residents still mount the occasional revue.

Tourism was a steady if unspectacular draw (because of its isolation, perhaps, or its Quaker heritage, Nantucket was never as showy as some of its mainland peers) from the late-19th century right up through the 1950s, when local businessman-benefactor Walter Beinecke, Jr., started spiffing up the waterfront for the

## Geography 101

*More than a few visitors debark from the ferries only to find themselves mildly disoriented. While it's true that the journey from Hyannis to Nantucket is pretty much southward, by the time the boat rounds Brandt Point to enter the harbor, it's facing due west. Main Street, at the core of the historic district, has an east–west orientation, stemming from Straight Wharf out to Madaket Road, which proceeds 6 mi west to Madaket Beach. Milestone Road, accessed from a rotary at the end of Orange Street off Main Street, is a straight, 8-mi shot to the easternmost town of 'Sconset (formally, Siasconset).*

*To find your way to the south-shore beaches or among the hillocks of Polpis—Altar Rock is the island's highest point, at a mere 100 ft—you'll want to use a map. The bike shops along the piers and the Nantucket Visitor Services and Information Bureau, at 25 Federal Street in the center of town, offer a useful assortment of maps for free.*

carriage trade. Since then, tourism has really taken off, becoming the island's bread and butter.

Like the original settlers and the early waves of tourists, most people who visit Nantucket today come to escape—from cities, from stress, and in some ways from the mayhem of the new millennium. Nantucket has a bit of nightlife, including two raucous year-round dance clubs, but that's not what the island is about. It's about small, gray-shingle cottages covered with pink roses in summer, about daffodil-lined roads in spring. It's about moors swept with brisk salt breezes and scented with bayberry and wild roses. Perhaps most of all, it's about rediscovering a quiet place within yourself and within the world, getting back in touch with the elemental and taking it home with you when you go.

# FOGGY MOORS, WINDSWEPT SHORES

Nantucket's reputation for enveloping fog—the reason sailors dubbed it "The Grey Lady" centuries back—is perhaps a bit exaggerated. The problem is not so much that the fog is omnipresent but that it can sweep in so quickly, obscuring sight lines and landmarks in a matter of minutes. The upside is that even if one beach is clouded over, you may well find the other side of the island bathed in radiant sunshine.

Island habitués appreciate the weather's fickleness. The moor you're biking through, one moment a patchwork of variegated green, can segue subtly to purplish gray; the moss and lichen clinging to the stunted pines and scrub oak (salt winds inhibit much growth outside the protective confines of town) loom up as if phosphorescent. Another benefit of the moisture-laden, Gulf Stream–borne air is a year-round differential from mainland temperatures of about 10 degrees: Nantucket is warmer in winter (snow doesn't stick around long, and some Mediterranean plants make it through), refreshingly cooler in summer.

As a glance at old maps or close observation of a single beach will attest, the island's very shape is similarly subject to constant change. Pounded by ocean waves, the south shore is steadily if slowly eroding, and the island's western and eastern tips are particularly exposed. In just the past decade, the sea has sheared off an entire 'Sconset beach, along with its low-lying houses; the structures remaining, including picturesque Sankaty Light, teeter at the brink of a high bluff. Countermeasures such as geotubes, installed to stabilize the sand, are generally acknowledged to be mere holding measures. What the ocean wants it will claim, heedless of our puny human powers.

Like the shoreline, the sand under the sea is always in motion. The shifting shoals off Nantucket have grounded hundreds of vessels—most notoriously the ocean liner *Andrea Doria* in 1954.

Sophisticated navigation devices seem to be no match for the vagaries of the waves. As recently as 1999, a cruise ship bound from Bermuda made an unscheduled offshore stopover of several days' duration.

Insistent currents can be a hazard for smaller craft. Amateur kayakers can, for instance, easily paddle across Nantucket Harbor to explore the scalloped coves of Coatue, a 4-mi barrier beach. Attempt a similar distance from westerly Smith's Point to the tiny islands of Tuckernuck and Muskeget beyond, however, and you could be in for the struggle of your life.

Nantucket's surf, particularly in the wake of storms, is not to be taken lightly. Whereas the northerly, sound-side beaches, from Children's past Jetties to Dionis, are nearly always placid, with knee-high waves that wouldn't topple a toddler, the ocean-side beaches are known for their "rollers," big round waves that will lift you off your feet (if you see one about to break, dive under it or you could get seriously pounded). The outer beaches, such as Madaket and 'Sconset, present further challenges with strong sidelong currents. And don't forget, the water is cold, peaking in the mid-70s by late summer.

If you're afraid to dip a toe in, much less bodysurf, there's plenty of pleasure to be had walking along the beach, poking about for scallop shells, moon snails, and "mermaid's purses" (the leathery egg sacs of harmless sand sharks). Just a few caveats: in approaching the beach, stick to the middle of a well-established path, and never walk through the dune grass. Not only are these spindly fronds a prime hangout for Lyme disease–carrying ticks (which ought to be disincentive enough), but their vast unseen networks of roots are all that's holding the sand in place. Even minimal damage can take a decade or more to undo.

Plain and hardy as it might seem, Nantucket's ecology is delicate—and already overstressed. The Nature Conservancy estimates that the islands of Nantucket and Martha's Vineyard represent 90% of the world's remaining sand-plain grassland; the rest has fallen

## Melville and Nantucket's Whaling Tradition

Surprisingly, Herman Melville had no firsthand knowledge of Nantucket when he set out to write Moby-Dick. In fact, he didn't visit the island until 1855, a year after the book was published. By that time, Capt. George Pollard, Jr., who had experienced the whale attack that inspired Melville's tale, was an old man who roamed the quiet streets as night watchman. What Melville did know, having himself shipped out on a whaler from New Bedford (he called it "my Harvard and my Yale"), was just how grueling these voyages could be.

Nantucket's preeminence as the world's whaling capital (at least until the early 1800s, when New Bedford's deeper harbor took the lead) resulted from a fluke, when, in 1712, Capt. Christopher Hussey's crew speared a sperm whale. The whale's waxy spermaceti, it was found, could be used for candles in place of lantern oil, produced by the messy, endless task of cooking down whale blubber. Hence, the chase was on: Nantucket's whaling fleet spread all the way to the Orient in search of "greasy luck."

Barring pirate and military attacks, shipwrecks and other acts of God, and the certainty of vermin and scurvy on the interminably long voyages, the captains made out like bandits: their grand houses still stand as proof. The crews had a harder time of it, but whaling had its advantages. It was virtually the only trade open to all races (hands were tough to sign on, with good reason), as well as one of the few offering a chance of upward mobility. Survive enough outings, and a diligent cabin boy might work his way up to captain.

The trade went into a downward spiral with the discovery of petroleum in 1836 and the commercial introduction of kerosene in 1959. Nantucket's fleet limped on a while longer, but the glory days were over—and so, too, was the seemingly limitless supply of stock. Today, there are thought to be fewer than 300 right whales in the Atlantic, and they're vulnerable to ever-increasing marine traffic. We may not have them around much longer—another thing Melville couldn't have known.

prey to industry and development. This particular habitat, besides being extraordinarily beautiful, supports a great variety of wildflowers and plants, some on the brink of extinction and others perhaps as yet unidentified. The scrubby heaths, threatened by a monoculture of invasive pines and scrub oaks, is crucial to the survival of species such as the Northern Harrier and short-eared owl. A consortium of conservation groups are taking steps to preserve the moors.

Nantucket's beaches are an important breeding ground for the endangered piping plover, a tiny speckled shorebird whose eggs, dropped right in the sand, resemble tiny pebbles. Every summer, Smith's Point is cordoned off to give a few dozen survivors the chance to fledge—much to the chagrin of some locals, whose pickups sport bumper stickers proclaiming "Piping Plovers Taste Just Like Chicken." Just as shocking—at least to the eco-concerned citizens, such as *Boston Globe* science writer Sy Montgomery, who confirmed that "a stretch of 'barren' beach can support millions of hidden lives"—are the beach-driving permits you'll see plastered on thousands of SUVs. Permits are cheap and easy to obtain. The same can't be said for the invaluable beauties and benefits of a rare setting left in peace.

## BETTER HOMES AND GARDENS

If gardening were a competitive sport—and from a quick tour around the island you'd swear it was—Nantucket would be a world contender. The relatively mild climate (for New England) compensates for rather poor, sandy soil and permits a growing season that lasts a good six months. Though not everyone can build a multimillion-dollar house, anyone can garden, and on Nantucket almost everyone does. Lovingly tended, a tiny cottage—such as the rose-festooned former fishing shacks of 'Sconset—can easily outshine a mega-mansion manned by a small army of landscapers. Gardening is a great leveler, capable of creating common ground across the island and islanders.

The season—social as well as horticultural—officially starts with Daffodil Weekend in late April, a beloved tradition of several decades' standing (☞ Nantucket Garden Club *in* Here and There). Jean McAusland, a former *House & Garden* editor, decided in the 1970s to beautify the island and plant hundreds of hardy daffodil bulbs. Admirers soon followed suit, and now some 3 million blooms line the roadways every spring. The weekend is invariably a sellout among the restaurants and inns, who open early to accommodate the crowds. Meanwhile, in the former ballroom of the old Point Breeze Hotel, the Nantucket Garden Club mounts a show of prize-worthy blossoms. If you think a daffodil is a daffodil, prepare to be amazed by the infinite variations in size, shape, and hue.

Soon the roses follow. The wild Rosa rugosa, or saltspray rose, rumored to have made its way here via China trade ships, prospers everywhere, under the most adverse circumstances, and produces blooms ranging from white to hot pink. The pasture, or Carolina, rose is the only legitimate native, but its ranks have been supplemented by such "volunteers" (garden-speak for cultivars turned runaways) as the Multiflora. On Rose Sunday in early July—a tradition just as treasured as Daffodil Weekend—the Congregational Church is lavished with rambling roses for a pops concert that is always packed.

You can spot a lot of magazine-worthy spreads just wandering around town. In many instances, the clever use of trellises can convert an entire house into a living 3D display. For a glimpse of some spectacular "secret gardens," sign on for one of the benefit house-and-garden tours (the hot ticket is St. Paul's in mid-July). They offer a chance to check out your neighbors' private backyards—and have a peek at some rarefied Nantucket interiors, themselves the subject of many a glossy coffee-table book.

In recent decades, however, there has been a trend to gut centuries-old interiors, rendering them more modern and leaving the

## Nantucket Reds

*Bermuda has its shorts, Fiji its sarongs. Nantucket's totemic clothing items are made of cotton dyed red so as to fade to a dull salmon shade. The reds were something of a secret code until they were singled out by* The Official Preppy Handbook *in 1980: "By their pink shirts ye shall know them" might be the watchwords for Nantucketers among the worldwide sailing community. Now reds are as site-specific as Martha's Vineyard's Black Dog line.*

*The principal purveyor is Murray's Toggery Shop on Main Street, which has catered to conservative dressers since the early 1900s. (Roland Macy worked here at his father's shop in the early 1800s before setting off to rewrite retailing history.) From baby togs to tote bags, you'll find everything you could want here in the way of reds. But for that weathered look that sets them off so well, you'll have to get out on the water.*

facades intact, or even rebuilding right down to the beams and rafters, all the while paying lip service to the stringent codes of the Historic District Commission. The result is a scattering of costly pseudo-historical nullities, mere architectural simulacra. Stricter regulations are under discussion, and sheer peer pressure may begin to chip away at the insidious newer-and-bigger-is-better mystique.

It's worth visiting some of the properties under the protection of the Nantucket Historical Society to get a sense of the way people used to live—quite nicely, it seems, without gymnasium-size rooms. Instead what islanders have always held in common is an appreciation for and attraction to the outdoors. A love of nature, rather than "house pride," is what keeps them out weeding and watering through the hot dry spells of late summer. It's what sends them biking and hiking all around the island to see what charming tableaux nature has fashioned entirely on its own.

## FROM JET-SETTERS TO CLAM SHUCKERS

Despite the escalating hype, Nantucket is not just the Hamptons squared. Yes, there is high society here (there always has been), but until very recently the preferred lifestyle was one of inconspicuous consumption—reverse snobbery, if you prefer. In August you'd see the vacationing bankers trading in their gray flannel suits for fishing gear and going about their business looking like blissful bums. Now that you can find any number of high-end boutiques in town but not a single hardware store, the tenor of daily life has subtly and perhaps irrevocably changed. It's easy enough to acquire the emblems of belonging (a suitably battered lightship basket purse, perhaps, or whale-embroidered cords), yet the essence remains elusive. Nantucket's quaint Christmas Stroll, as much a chance to meet and greet as shop, is increasingly awash in minks, and the citizenry is understandably nonplussed. Who are these people, you can almost hear the year-rounders wondering, and what do they want from us?

Everyone, it seems, from the day-trippers who are happy to head home with a souvenir T-shirt to the gazillionaires who debark from their yachts for a three-digit dinner, just wants a little piece of "The Rock"—the fond nickname given the isle by those familiar with its harsh winter face. Of course, the longer you stick around and the fewer demands you make on the island, the better your odds that it will speak to you. For many, the message is this: keep coming back.

Among those who have heeded the call are summering intelligentsia, such as journalist Russell Baker (who hosts PBS's *Masterpiece Theatre*), historian David Halberstam, novelist Frank

## Kids and Dogs

*Forgive the lumping of categories: it's just that Nantucket is a paradise for the young and restless, be they human or canine. Take a seat at one of the benches along Main Street to catch the passing parade—gaggles of towheads in Tevas™ bound for an ice cream cone at one of two neighboring drugstore fountains, plus a veritable Westminster Show of handsome dogs. Appearances notwithstanding, golden retrievers are not required accessories, but they're certainly prized. And just as little children can claim their own dedicated beach complete with playground and bandstand—called Children's, naturally enough—dogs have several special stomping and romping grounds, including Tuppancy Links, a converted golf course overlooking the sound, and recourse to the $4 million MSPCA facility, which could pass for a trophy house.*

Conroy, composer Ned Rorem, children's book editor Margaret McElderry—and that's just a sampling of the growing roster. Just last year, Nathaniel Philbrick, whose name is among the island's oldest, turned his research at the Nantucket Historical Association into a book that earned a million-dollar advance, an excerpt in *Vanity Fair*, and a slot on the *New York Times* best-seller list. *Jaws* author Peter Benchley—whose grandfather, actor-critic and Algonquin Round Table wit Robert Benchley, discovered 'Sconset in 1922, when it was in full flower as an actors' colony—best defined the island's lure for creative types in a *Today* show segment in 1976: "Nantucket is, basically, a state of mind," he said, "where various people who come or live here do so because they feel they can find something. Their success is in direct proportion to what they themselves bring."

Raised in Nantucket, Jonathan Burkhart and Jill Goode (a thirty-something brother-sister pair) ventured into the independent film world, prospered, and brought that world here, with the first Nantucket Film Festival in 1996. Every June you can count on a flurry of star sightings. The opportunity to view the coming year's most intriguing releases is appealing, as are the invitation-only parties (though security is getting perhaps a bit too tight: during the fifth festival Burkhart and Goode found themselves barred from a fete). The real excitement is the chance to participate in discussions led by Jace Alexander (the actor-director son of a noted 'Sconset couple, TV producer Ed Sherin and actress Jane Alexander, a former director of the National Endowment of Arts) or to see the comedy duo of Anne Meara and Jerry Stiller, long-time Brant Point summerers, kibitz and kick loose in a staged reading of an original screenplay.

Later in the summer, other celebs move in—fashion moguls such as Tommy Hilfiger and Chanel USA CEO Arie Kopelman; "Juice Guys" Tom First and Tom Scott of Nantucket Nectars (who got their start peddling smoothies off Straight Wharf); luxury mall developer Stephen Karp, who also owns three of Nantucket's biggest hotels; Senator John Kerry and his philanthropic wife, Theresa Heinz; former Chrysler CEO Lee Iacocca, who's now promoting eco-friendly "E-bikes"—and that's not even mentioning the big shots who drop in semi-incognito. Bill Gates has been known to jet in from time to time for a round at the Nantucket Golf Club, where membership fees start at about a quarter-million. Bill Clinton played here, too, in 1999, and the First Couple enjoyed their initial day trip enough to return the next year for a low-key overnight.

However, the real notables here, if you ask any native, are the hard workers committed to the long haul—to improving the quality of island life, in-season and off: people like Helen Seager, who spearheaded efforts to restore the African Meeting House, or

Sara Alger, who as moderator manages the contentious factions at Town Meeting every year with a mix of sangfroid and good humor. In a small rural community such as this one, respect is a commodity not easily earned, and it certainly can't be bought—despite the flurry of dollars blowing around the island.

*"Perfect days" are, of course, a matter of personal preference. Yours, for instance, might involve reading a lengthy novel that keeps you strapped in a hammock all day or something more adventurous, in which time passes so quickly aboard a sailboat that approaching the dock at sunset is almost saddening. Each of the outings below covers one aspect of the island's best activities. Since they're all different, you can pick one that matches your inner beachcomber when you're feeling lazy or something more rigorous when you've closed the cover on* Middlemarch.

## In This Chapter



*By Sandy MacDonald*

# perfect days

## A PERFECT DAY ON THE WATER

Before a long journey at sea, you've got to rise early and fuel up. Provisions (☞ Eating Out) on Harbor Square is a great source for morning munchies and picnic stuff for the voyage out. After breakfast, head down to the Straight Wharf and wander about the slips to see which boat most appeals.

If you're not already a boat owner, you can board a beauty like the *Endeavor*, a replica Friendship sloop that sails out of Straight Wharf. You can join a group sail that leaves the wharf at set times; other crafts might be available for a private picnic-and-champagne charter to a cove along Coatue. Those sticking to a beer budget can always paddle out and have a picnic on the beach. Sea Nantucket rents kayaks and small sailboats at the vest-pocket Francis Street Beach, about ¼ mi southeast along Washington Street. The water here is usually calm enough for amateurs, but if you really want to learn the ropes and are here for several weeks, check out the courses offered by Nantucket Island Community Sailing. Another good place to try out water toys—kayaks, sailboards, and small sailboats—is broad and gentle Jetties Beach. (☞ For further information on boat trips and beaches, *see* Outdoor Activities and Sports).

To prolong your communion with the water into the evening, consider having dinner at RopeWalk or Straight Wharf (☞ Eating Out). Both are right on the harbor. Or go for the America's Cup of dining experiences and take a dinner cruise to the Wauwinet. The *Wauwinet Lady* will spirit you smoothly from Straight Wharf through the moorings—keeping the cocktails served en route steady—and 6 mi farther to the island's most luxurious resort for a superlative meal. On the way back you can count on an equally spectacular sunset.

## A NATURALIST'S PERFECT DAY

Any self-respecting naturalist will want to head out at dawn to see what the birds are up to. The Downyflake (☞ Eating Out), a homey mid-island breakfast joint, starts serving at 5:30 AM—a laggardly 6 AM on Sunday. Pick up a couple of homemade doughnuts for carbo-loading on the road.

The best way to bird is on bike (☞ Bike Shops *in* Outdoor Activities and Sports). Head a couple of miles west of Downyflake and past town to explore a 900-acre preserve comprising Sanford Farm, the Woods, and Ram Pasture, maintained by the Nantucket Conservation Foundation (☞ Outdoor Activities and Sports). To get to the preserve, take Cliff Road (consult a bike map available from the tourism office) to get to the start of the Madaket Bike Path (☞ Outdoor Activities and Sports). Then it's a scenic zigzag past the Old Mill. A few miles farther on the path, just before the intersection with Cliff Road, you'll see a roughhewn parking lot. From here (you'll have to ditch your bike—there's a place to lock it up), 6½ mi of hiking trails cross forest and meadow to reach pond and sea, wetlands, and rare sand-plain grassland (☞ Outdoor Activities and Sports)—all of Nantucket's distinctive habitats in succession. Figure on at least two hours of walking and gawking, more if you're an avid stalker.

After emerging from the preserve, the strong of leg may bike another 3 mi west along the bike path to Madaket Beach, pausing to pick up a picnic lunch at the Westender (☞ Eating Out), and plod onward along Smith's Point, where the endangered piping plovers dwell. (You will, of course, tread carefully and in no way harass them.) Then, head back into town and poke around the Maria Mitchell Association's natural history museum and library (☞ Here and There), where you can read up on the environs you've just explored. For dinner, retire to the India House (☞ Eating Out) a few blocks away, where you can dine in the lovely outdoor garden before swooping home on your bike through the cool, starry night.

## A PERFECT DAY FOR BIKING

It could easily be argued that every day is a perfect day for biking on Nantucket. Winter, summer, rain, or sun, Nantucket terrain seems custom-made for biking—never too steep and always scenic. Start with a hearty breakfast at the Rotary (☞ Eating Out), at the outset of Milestone Road about 1 mi southeast of the center of town. From here it's another 7 absolutely straight mi to 'Sconset, but plan to take your second left to get onto the Polpis Bike Path, the newest and prettiest in Nantucket's network.

On your right, about 3½ mi out, look for Altar Rock Road, a dirt track that will take you to the island's highest point (just past the weird '50s-futuristic weather station), which is also the nexus of the best mountain-biking trails. This area was common sheep pasturage during the 19th century. In other words, it's rocky and choppy, all the qualities dirtheads prize. The crimson fields to the southeast are actually cranberry bogs. You can eventually regain Milestone Road in that direction, but it's more rewarding to return to the Polpis Bike Path, which makes a leisurely loop past Sesachacha Pond and the iconic striped Sankaty Lighthouse (☞ Here and There). Clamber up to its base to see how precariously it's perched on the eroding bluff before you pull into the cluster of sea-beaten cottages that is 'Sconset. Pause at the Sconset Market (☞ Eating Out) for rarefied refreshments before heading back into town—straight along Milestone Road or back the way you came.

You probably still have a good half-day ahead of you, which is time enough and more to bike the other half of the island, out Madaket Road. Or you could rest your weary muscles, have a relaxed pub-style supper at the Brotherhood (☞ Eating Out), and head out again in the gloaming.

## A CULTURE VULTURE'S PERFECT DAY (OR, A PERFECT RAINY DAY)

It's really not the end of the world when blustery weather kicks in. For starters, a soggy day is always brightened by a cheery breakfast at Black-Eyed Susan's (☞ Eating Out). You stand a better chance of slipping in on the early side. After breakfast, window-shop the boutiques along Centre Street (a.k.a. Petticoat Row), ducking in and out of the dripping doorways, before heading down Broad Street to explore the Whaling Museum (☞ Here and There). You don't have to be a nautical nut or have kids with you to appreciate this well-presented repository, in a former spermaceti candle factory. Evocative exhibits such as a reconstructed tryworks (where whalers cooked down the blubber for lamp oil) summon the up- and downside of this daring pursuit that affected all aspects of Nantucket life. Stay long enough to catch one of the lectures and spring for a pass to all the Nantucket Historical Association sites; it's good for the whole season.

For lunch, what could be more appropriate than the aptly named Fog Island Cafe (☞ Eating Out)? On rainy days the two local theaters often show matinees: both are within a half-block of Fog Island. Or meander up Main Street, taking shelter in Wayne Pratt Antiques, Mitchell's Book Corner (paying special attention to the Nantucket Room), or one the unique art galleries (☞ Shopping). Then return to the center of town, where, at 21 Federal (☞ Eating Out), you can sip a thematic "Dark and Stormy" (ginger beer and rum) before settling in for a terrific dinner.

# A PERFECT WINTERY DAY

Every year-rounder will sooner or later confront the question "But what do you do here all winter?" And many an islander will undoubtedly reply, "Enjoy the peace and quiet." It's true that off-season options can appear limited and, to some eyes, tedious, but the daylight hours, though short, are rich with possibility.

Everyone tends to gravitate to Espresso café (☞ Eating Out) for morning coffee and whatnot—or maybe just the chance to catch sight of a few increasingly familiar faces. You'll see those same faces heading over to the post office on Federal Street to collect their mail, the Atheneum to check out new magazines and books, and perhaps poking about the few stores that remain open, like Murray's (☞ Shopping).

On all but a few of the fiercest days, winter is actually a great time for bike rides and beach walks. With traffic reduced to a trickle, you can bike all the pathless roads that might seem a bit too treacherous in summer: Eel Point, Hummock Pond, Wauwinet. As you walk along your perfectly private beach, keep an eye out for seals, which come here from Maine over the winter. You're virtually guaranteed sighting along the jetties (stone piers) at the harbor's mouth. You can walk out the west one, past Brant Point, when it's not too wet or slick.

You'll probably want to keep your outings brief, hightailing it back to town from time to time for sustenance at the few year-round places. The Fog Island Cafe (☞ Eating Out) makes a cozy stop for lunch. The tiny Centre Street Bistro (☞ Eating Out) is *the* spot for a delicious dinner, and this time of year, you can actually get in. In between, you might want to warm your toes and perhaps sip a hot toddy by the fire in the gracious parlor of the Jared Coffin House, which has seen generations through winters just as chilly (☞ Eating Out).

*Dining out in Nantucket is such a popular participatory sport that table talk—and impromptu inter-table talk—is apt to center on discussions of where one ate last, where one is planning to eat next, and what's been the best so far. "So far" is the operative term. With a score of top-tier restaurants intent on outdoing one another, the mantle never settles for long.*

## In This Chapter



*By Sandy MacDonald*

# eating out

**FOR SUCH A TINY ISLAND,** Nantucket is rife with great restaurants—"world class" would be no exaggeration. Of course, with New York–level sophistication comes New York–level prices. And whereas the titans of industry who flock here for a bit of high-rent R&R might not blink at the prospect of a $40 entrée, the rest of us must sometimes suppress a nervous gulp. Is it worth it? Again and again, in venues that vie for the title of most recherché, the answer is yes.

New American fever hit Nantucket about two decades ago and shows no signs of abating. Often, the chefs brought in to dazzle at established front-runners decide to stay on and open places of their own. Thus, the restaurant scene is constantly expanding and improving.

Even though the island itself isn't agriculturally equipped to furnish much more than a bit of produce and some homegrown herbs and greens (lovely as they can be), New England's top greengrocers are on tap to provide regional delicacies. The seafood, naturally, is nonpareil, especially local scallops in season.

So don't let the prices deter you. The general excellence of Nantucket's restaurants seems to have a trickle-down effect: even many of the more modest eateries pack unexpected panache.

## Prices

| CATEGORY | COST* |
|---|---|
| **$$$$** | over $50 |
| **$$$** | $35–$50 |
| **$$** | $25–$35 |
| **$** | under $25 |

**per person for a three-course meal, excluding drinks, service, and 5% sales tax*

## How and When

Reservations can be hard to come by in high season, as well as popular weekends such as December's Christmas Stroll and the Daffodil Festival in April, so plan well ahead. The better restaurants can get booked up weeks in advance, so reservations are always recommended. (We mention only when they're essential or not accepted.) Or consider alternative time slots: the odds will be in your favor if you're willing to eat unfashionably early or decadently late.

In any month other than July or August, call ahead to check hours of operation, which tend to shrink. Dining off-season used to be a dicey proposition, but in the past few years, enough talented resident chef-owners have set up shop so that the options even in the dead of winter can be mighty inviting. We list months closed; otherwise, it's safe to assume that places are open year-round.

If you're heading off-island and find you have a surfeit of groceries, they'd be greatly appreciated by the Nantucket Emergency Food Pantry at St. Paul's Church, 20 Fair Street (tel. 508/228–7438); other churches in town accept drop-off donations.

## DINING IN NANTUCKET TOWN

**$$$$** ★ **THE PEARL.** Nantucket has never seen the likes of this ultracool space, shoehorned by New York City designer Chris Smith (Nobu

## Days of Wine and Roses

*Founded in 1997 by Le Languedoc sommelier Denis Toner, the Nantucket Wine Festival enlivens late May with a weekend-long roundelay of lectures and seminars, private soirees within elegant houses, a wine auction at the Chanticleer, grand tastings at the Sconset Casino (more than 125 vintners from around the world contribute), and a choice of winery dinners at top restaurants. This party's not for oenophiles only: the event celebrates Nantucket's long-lived and ever more ardent love affair with gastronomy as a whole.*

*"We like to think that the Wine Festival is an overture to the dining season on Nantucket," Toner told the local magazine* Your Nantucket Holiday *on the occasion of the millennial festival. "It is a celebration of our gustatory resources, our uniqueness as a culinary microclimate. Nantucket has a very high density of great restaurants."*

et al.) into the shell of a modest clapboard house whose basement contains the Boarding House (☞ *below*), Seth and Angela Raynor's original restaurant. The uptown setting upstairs is seriously chic, with a white onyx bar lit a Curaçao blue and, behind an aquarium divider, cushy banquettes of pearl leather. These—plus the garden porch where tasting dinners can be prearranged—are the power seats. However, everyone is well served by Seth's enthusiasm for clarion flavors, often delivered with an Asian or Mediterranean twist. Consider the oyster shooters (accompaniments range from *ponzu*, a lemony soy-based sauce, to basil oil) or the masterful sautéed foie gras with caramelized mango—and these are just the appetizers. For truly exciting cuisine, at somewhat dizzying prices,

# nantucket town dining

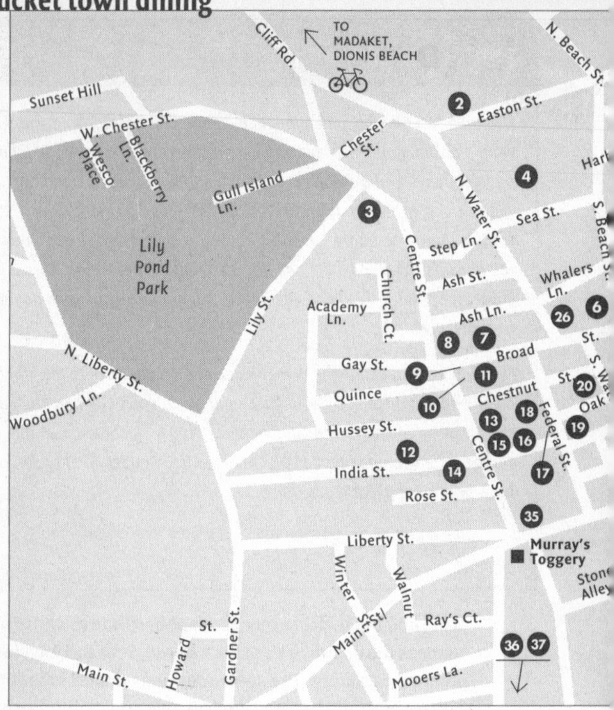


American Bounty, 39
American Seasons, 3
Arno's, 35
The Atlantic Cafe, 24
Black-Eyed Susan's, 14
The Boarding House, 17
Bosun's Bistro, 33
Brant Point Grill, 1
Brotherhood of Thieves, 7
Cambridge Street, 25
Cap'n Tobey's Chowder House, 32
Centre Street Bistro, 13
Chancellor's, 2
Cioppino's, 11
The Club Car, 27
Company of the Cauldron, 16
DeMarco, 15
Fifty-Six Union, 38
Fog Island Café, 26
The Food Fare at the Harbor House, 4
India House, 12
Jared's, 8
Kendrick's, 10
Le Languedoc, 9
The Nantucket Lobster Trap, 34
Nantucket Tapas, 5

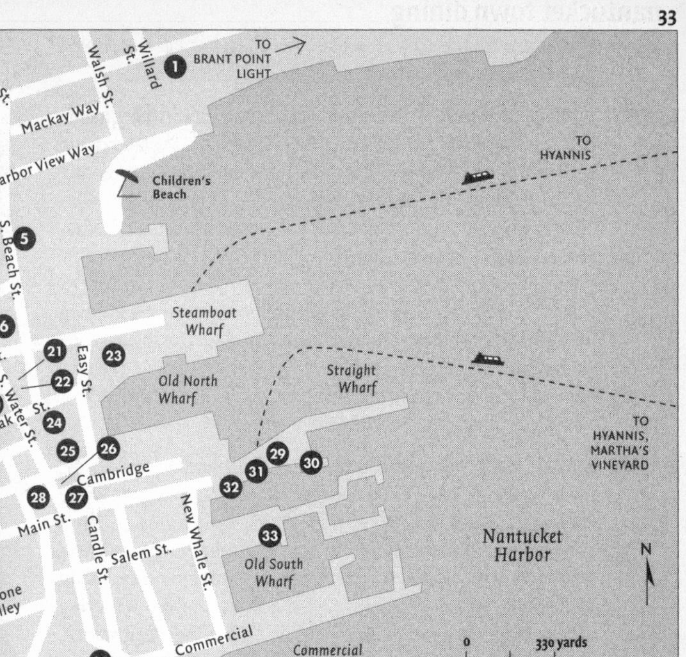


Oran Mor, **6**
the pearl, **18**
RopeWalk, **30**
Rose & Crown Pub, **21**
Schooners, **23**
Ships Inn, **36**
Straight Wharf, **29**
Sushi by Yoshi, **20**
The Tap Room, **8**
The Tavern, **31**
21 Federal, **19**
The Woodbox, **37**
Vincent's, **22**
White Dog Cafe, **28**

this is the place to patronize. Reservations are strongly recommended. *12 Federal St., tel. 508/228–9701. AE, MC, V.*

$$$$ **STRAIGHT WHARF.** This sail loft–like restaurant with harborside deck has enjoyed legendary status for two decades. The latest hand at the helm, since 1995, is that of executive chef Steve Cavagnaro, who immediately inspires confidence with an intense and briny lobster bisque. Promise is upheld in such dishes as polenta-crusted local sea scallops with a corn, chanterelle, and oyster sauce. Everything, from cuisine to service, is just right, if on the pricey side. If you'd like a preview, try the café menu at the adjoining bar—that is, if you can get in. It becomes quite the social scene as the evening progresses. Reservations are recommended for dinner. *6 Harbor Sq., Straight Wharf, tel. 508/228–4499. AE, MC, V. Closed Labor Day–Memorial Day. No lunch.*

$$$–$$$$ **BRANT POINT GRILL.** With its beautiful broad lawn set harborside, the Brant Point Grill—in-house restaurant for the elegant White Elephant hotel (☞ Where to Stay)—purports to be a straightforward, albeit top-dollar source of prime meats and fish. It's that and more. You'll be tempted by the salmon smoked in plain sight, on cedar planks poised downwind from a blazing brazier. But be sure to try the more subtle stuff as well: for instance, the duck in vanilla rum glaze (yum) or the sweet cranberry Portuguese bread pudding. As for the grand breakfast buffet, prepare to be blown away. Reservations are recommended. *50 Easton St., tel. 508/325–1320. AE, D, DC, MC, V. No smoking. Closed Oct.–May. www.brantpointgrill.com*

$$$–$$$$ **CIOPPINO'S.** A former maître d' at the Chanticleer (☞ *below*), Tracy Root had a clear calling as restaurateur. His own place has been popular since day one (in 1991), thanks to his knack for making patrons feel pampered yet at ease. Beyond the signature dish—a San Franciscan seafood stew served over linguine—the menu is quite ambitious, marrying classic technique and brave new ingredients. (Consider the grilled sea bass with peach chile

sauce and smoked mango relish.) Desserts, including an irresistible tiramisu, have their own following: it's especially pleasant to stop in at the patio late in the evening for a light and convivial, if caloric, bite. The interior is quietly elegant, lending an instant aura of special occasion. *20 Broad St., tel. 508/228–4622. D, DC, MC, V. No smoking. Closed Oct.–Mar. www.cioppinos.com*

**$$$–$$$$** **THE CLUB CAR.** A long-time favorite among the moneyed set, this boxy dining room—its piano bar is an actual railroad car from the dismantled 'Sconset narrow-gauge—has never quite shaken its Continental origins, for which read occasionally salty sauces. Richness, however, has its own rewards, as in a plump double-cut slab of swordfish rolled in moisture-retaining crushed almonds and walnuts, topped with pecan butter. As for the "Opera Cake"—a kind of stand-up tiramisu—tradition never tasted so good. Reservations are recommended. *1 Main St., tel. 508/228–1101. MC, V. No smoking. Closed Jan.–Apr. www.theclubcar.com*

**$$$–$$$$** **DEMARCO.** Northern Italian cuisine debuted on-island at this cored-out clapboard house in 1980, slightly ahead of the wave. The delights endure: "badly cut" homemade pasta, for instance, in a sauce of wild mushrooms, prosciutto, and fresh sage, or braised lamb served atop Parmesan polenta custard. Of late, however, owner Don DeMarco has begun tweaking the menu to cater to today's playful, global leanings. The result? The best of both worlds. *9 India St., tel. 508/228–1836. AE, MC, V. No smoking. Closed Nov.–Apr. No lunch. www.nantucket.net/food/demarco*

**$$$–$$$$** **FIFTY-SIX UNION.** This onetime diner, a pleasant walk from the center of town, got a chic millennial makeover: now there's no mistaking its intended niche. Chef-owner Peter Jannelle provides light, healthy fare with the international trimmings Nantucketers favor: a grilled quail salad, for instance, with Asian greens and Belgian endive, and Javanese spicy fried rice. Reservations are recommended. *56 Union St., tel. 508/228–6135. AE, MC, V. No smoking. No lunch.*

**$$$–$$$$ LE LANGUEDOC.** The name notwithstanding, this multifaceted restaurant, founded in 1975, long ago cast off Gallic convention to embrace new American eclecticism. There are three ways to enjoy the kitchen's output, in ascending order of expense: in the garden patio (a perfect place to drop in for tapas or dessert); off the café menu, in the cheery basement bistro; and in the formal dining rooms (one of which is a crimson-painted knockout). Every level satisfies. Locals especially appreciate the café in a town where prices are not always kind. Reservations are recommended for the upstairs dining rooms. *24 Broad St., tel. 508/228–2552. AE, MC, V. No smoking. Closed Jan.–mid-Apr. No lunch. www.lelanguedoc.com*

**$$$–$$$$ THE NANTUCKET LOBSTER TRAP.** You might not care much for the atmosphere at this fairly standard fish house with conventional offerings (bacon-wrapped scallops, stuffed quahogs, etc.). The ubiquity of TV screens gives it a sports-bar ambience—although no one seems to mind. *25 Washington St., tel. 508/228–4200. AE, MC, V. Closed Nov.–Apr. No lunch.*

**$$$–$$$$ ORAN MOR.** Chef-owner Peter Wallace ascended to this tastefully appointed second-story eatery—named for a prized single-malt Scotch—by way of Topper's at the Wauwinet (☞ *below*), which should give some indication of the hauteness of the endeavor. Not every dish delivers, but it's always worth the gamble. Opt if possible for the front room, with its splashes of harbor view past the Yacht Club. *2 S. Beach St., tel. 508/228–8655. AE, MC, V. No smoking. Closed Mon. No lunch weekdays.*

**$$$–$$$$ SHIPS INN.** Tucked into the *rez-de-chaussée* (first floor) of Captain Obed Starbuck's handsome 1831 mansion, this peach-tint, candlelit restaurant is a light and lovely haven wherein French cuisine meets a California sensibility and both cultures are the richer for it. If you want to eat healthy, you can: there's nothing sinful about the chilled lobster consommé, for instance, other than its exquisite flavor.

At the beginning of the meal, you can promise yourself a blowout ending in the form of the soufflé du jour. In between, try grilled whole yellowtail flounder with ginger beurre blanc, perhaps, or scallops with chive-sorrel risotto. Anyone missing chef Mark Gottwald's touch off-season can always track him down in Vero Beach, Florida, where it's on-season for his other restaurant, Ellie's, named for his wife. *13 Fair St., tel. 508/228–0040. AE, MC, V. No smoking. Closed Nov.–Mar. No lunch. www.nantucket.net/lodging/shipsinn*

**$$$–$$$$** ★ **21 FEDERAL.** An avatar of the new American revolution since 1985, 21 Federal retains its creative edge, thanks to the ever-avant menus of chef Russell Jaehnig. Nothing is outré, mind you, in this handsome 1847 Greek Revival house with sconce-lit, dove-gray interiors. But the food has a spark to match the spirited clientele (some of the celebrated bar's bonhomie invariably spills over). Sautéed softshell crabs, when in season, turn up with saffron fennel salad, and swordfish is imaginatively paired with mole sauce, salsa, and corn pudding (unbelievably, it works). Despite the price wars currently raging about town, convivial hands-on owner Chick Walsh has managed to hold the line at a reasonable level while never letting quality flag. *21 Federal St., tel. 508/228–2121. AE, MC, V. No smoking. Closed Jan.–Mar. www.21federal.net*

**$$$** **AMERICAN BOUNTY.** A tiny restaurant tucked into the Tuckernuck Inn (☞ Where to Stay), American Bounty enjoys good local buzz for its relatively modest prices. Chef John Cataldi manages small miracles, such as an appetizer of bay scallops with truffle oil and asparagus, and most entrées are available in half portions. The decor—lots of whitewashed latticework—lends itself better to breakfast, which is also a find. Reservations are recommended for dinner. *60 Union St., tel. 508/228–3886. AE, DC, MC, V. No smoking. Closed Nov.–Apr. No lunch. www.tuckernuckinn.com*

**$$$** ★ **AMERICAN SEASONS.** At once playful and tasteful, this intimate space arrayed with folk art—you'll be dining on a lacquered game table—is commensurately romantic. It's not just the subdued lighting and smooth service. Chef-owner Michael Getter's dishes—on the grand side and festively presented—explore the continental United States, from the Pacific Coast to New England, by way of the Wild West and Down South, so that any type of craving you have can probably be accommodated. Tuna tempura, Hudson Valley foie gras, grilled Wyoming trout, crayfish ravioli . . . expect heart-warming pan-regional pyrotechnics. *80 Centre St., tel. 508/228–7111. Reservations essential. AE, MC, V. No smoking. Closed late Dec.–May. No lunch. www.americanseasons.com*

$$$ ★ **BLACK-EYED SUSAN'S.** From a passing glance, you'd never peg this seemingly humble storefront as one of Nantucket's more chic eateries—but it is. The corny wood paneling is offset by improbably fancy glass chandeliers, and foodies lay claim to the stools at the former lunch counter to observe chef Jess Worster's "open kitchen." The dinner menu, which changes every three weeks, ventures boldly around the world and never lacks for novelty or finesse. The breakfasts—served until 1 PM for the matutinally challenged—are just as stellar, featuring such eye-openers as sourdough French toast with orange Jack Daniels butter and pecans. *10 India St., tel. 508/325–0308. No credit cards. No smoking. Closed Nov.–Apr. No dinner Sun. No lunch.*

$$$ **THE BOARDING HOUSE.** Beyond the throngs of madly mingling twentysomethings—the bar is extremely popular—you'll encounter a culinary oasis, a semi-subterranean space lined with vaguely Mediterranean murals, where chef-owner Seth Raynor showcases his skill with both European and Asian cuisine, and then blends them into New American masterpieces. The lively offerings here, such as the fragrant shellfish stew or grilled brace of Szechuan quail, are served in enormous portions (and bowls) are a bit more traditional than those at the Pearl (☞ *above*), his latest venture upstairs, but every bit as good and a bit more affordable. The café menu, served on the sidewalk patio in summer, is less costly, too,

but good luck getting a table; everyone with any taste has already had the same bright idea. Of considerable consolation to locals is the Boarding House's commitment to staying open year-round. *12 Federal St., tel. 508/228–9622. AE, MC, V. No smoking.*

**$$$ COMPANY OF THE CAULDRON.** A beloved institution since the mid-'70s, the Cauldron is unique among Nantucket restaurants. The tiny dining room, a sconce-lit haven of handsome architectural salvage, is served by an even smaller kitchen, whence chef-owner All Kovalencik issues extraordinary prix-fixe dinners night after night. There's only one menu per evening, but adepts gladly forego multiple-choice when the chef's choice is invariably so dead-on. (Rundowns of the weekly roster are available over the phone or on-line.) You might encounter the likes of chilled white gazpacho with sliced lobster and fresh basil, or fork-tender chateaubriand. You might come away better acquainted with your near neighbors, too: the Cauldron is like a select dinner party where the guests are self-invited. *7 India St., tel. 508/228–4016. Reservations essential. MC, V. No smoking. Closed Nov.–May. No lunch. www.companyofthecauldron.com*

**$$$ INDIA HOUSE.** The small, simple rooms of a 1750s house, a residential block removed from the sometimes hectic center of town, make a splendid setting for fanciful, forward-looking meals. Chef Rita Tyler, who gained a rapt following at the even older Woodbox (☞ *below*), dishes up bold world cuisine, such as curried shrimp and clams with wild rice waffles, and grilled swordfish caponata (a relish of eggplant, olives, and other ingredients). All the inventiveness rests on a firm foundation of classical technique. And try the Sunday brunch, if only to experience "Mango Margarita Madness." *37 India St., tel. 508/228–9043. Reservations essential. AE, D, MC, V. No smoking. Closed Dec.–Apr. No lunch.*

**$$$ JARED'S.** In the Jared Coffin House's (☞ Where to Sleep) formal restaurant, stiff family portraits and blustery nautical paintings overlook a calm sea of Queen Anne–style chairs. In a room so clearly catering to traditional tastes, the menu reads as borderline seditious—seductive, at any rate. Imagine Malpeque oysters accompanied by a granita of cantaloupe and blood oranges, or a shelled lobster aswim in champagne basil cream sauce. Breakfasts are comparably formal and rich. *29 Broad St., tel. 508/228–2400. AE, D, DC, MC, V. No smoking. No lunch. www.jaredcoffinhouse.net*

$$$ **KENDRICK'S.** Less flashy than some of its neighboring competitors, this tiny restaurant—a cluster of whitewashed rooms behind mullioned glass—delivers big-time flavors: seared foie gras, for instance, served with Royal Gala apple butter, or mildly tart, exquisitely juicy honey-lime marinated salmon. Locals in the know mix with transients lucky enough to happen upon this little gem. Not everyone knows about breakfast, either, and is thus missing out on the challah French toast with sautéed bananas and rum raisins. *5 Chestnut St., tel. 508/228–9156. AE, D, MC, V. Closed Jan.–Mar. www.thequakerhouse.com.*

$$$ **ROPEWALK.** It's time to revise that tired old axiom of coastal living, that you can never find good food right on the water. Here at the very end of Straight Wharf (go any farther and you'll be boarding someone's yacht), both setting and cooking are excellent. The chowder is exemplary (creamy but not gummy), and the grilled shrimp and spinach salad with julienned vegetables and orange-sesame dressing is the very model of a perfect summer meal. *1 Straight Wharf, tel. 508/228–8886. MC, V. Closed Nov.–Apr. www.theropewalk.com*

$$$ **THE WOODBOX.** Antiquity meets a modernist culinary sensibility in this 1709 house complete with its original "keeping room," or kitchen—the prize among three very lovely wattle-and-daub dining rooms. A parade of gifted chefs have passed through these portals over the decades, all with excellent pedigrees; several have gone into business for themselves. The current team lives up to the tradition, offering such sophisticated

concoctions as a foie gras pâté paired with a malted berry sauce and blueberry-caramel compote, and seared rare ahi tuna with pineapple risotto. Regulars would rebel if the signature beef Wellington were ever to be dropped, but rest assured that this one is state-of-the-art. *29 Fair St., tel. 508/228–0587. Reservations essential. No credit cards. No smoking. Closed Mon. and Jan.–Apr. No lunch. www.woodboxinn.com*

**$$–$$$** **ARNO'S.** Arno's makes optimal use of its prime location right on Main Street to present lush breakfasts (as in a lobster and goat cheese omlette), hearty lunches (particularly the daily soup-and-sandwich deal), and respectably ambitious dinners (such as the shrimp and sirloin combo and the phyllo-wrapped salmon. Mind you, you may not be dazzled; neither will you be disappointed. Molly Dee's nostalgic canvases adorn the brick walls. Expect some envious looks—from within and without—if you get to sit near the storefront windows. *41 Main St., tel. 508/228–7001. AE, D, MC, V. No smoking. Closed Jan.–Mar.*

**$$–$$$** **THE ATLANTIC CAFE.** Long popular with visitors and locals alike for fairly predictable bar food, the AC has begun adding little flourishes, such as gnocchi sauced with cream, asparagus, and oyster mushrooms, and sea scallops paired with ricotta-crab ravioli. The nautical flotsam that represents the bulk of the decor is not some decorator's scheme but vestiges of the real thing. *15 S. Water St., tel. 508/228–0570. AE, D, DC, MC, V. No smoking. www.atlanticcafe.com*

**$$–$$$** **BOSUN'S BISTRO.** Occupying an awning-covered patio at the end of picturesque South Wharf, this seasonal eatery redefines festive. It's not just the lavish flower boxes (whose blooms adorn many a plate), or the free live jazz brought in to enliven weekday nights. From breakfast through dinner, chef James Gee's approach is light and vivid. Entrées follow a general pattern: generous portions of meat or fish propped atop variously flavored pilafs or pastas and subjected to a confetti of multicolor peppers, parsley, and tiny purple flowers. Every plate makes you feel as if it's your birthday—and if that doesn't do the trick, try the fantastic tiramisu cake. 14 *Old South Wharf, tel. 508/228–7774. AE, MC, V. Closed Nov.–Apr.*

$$–$$$ **CAMBRIDGE STREET.** This in-town storefront started out primarily as a bar—and the original room, painted midnight-blue, is still ideal for spirited mixing—but chef-owner Brandt Gould's open-grill international fusion cuisine proved so popular, a quieter nook had to be added on. Even the most jaded of palates will thrill to this pan-Asian–barbecue–Middle Eastern melange. All ages and strata come here to be shaken *and* stirred, and never, ever gouged. 12 *Cambridge St., tel. 508/228–7109. AE, D, DC, MC, V. No smoking. Closed Jan.–Mar. No lunch.*

$$–$$$ ★ **CENTRE STREET BISTRO.** Tiny—there are only 20 seats indoors, and even fewer out—and perfect, this gem of a bistro is a find that devoted locals almost wish they could keep to themselves. Having honed their chops at the celebrated Summer House (☞ Where to Stay) in 'Sconset, chef-owners Tim and Ruth Pitts provide an astounding three meals a day and stay open year-round (cutting back a bit in the slow season). The menu evolves throughout the year, but a reliable favorite is the shrimp and rice-noodle stir-fry with Thai curry and cilantro. The desserts depend on inspiration and invariably receive it. 29 *Centre St., tel. 508/228–8470. No credit cards.*

$$–$$$ **CHANCELLOR'S.** A once-grand hotel, built in 1891, the Point Breeze has seen better days and is starting to again, thanks to the timely ministrations of the new owners, the Gonnella family. Its dining hall—a former basketball court—has been freshened up and reconfigured to foster intimacy. The menu is meant to encompass family to fine dining and, amazingly, succeeds: the steamed mussels sparked with Triple Sec and cilantro and the soy-lacquered salmon with gingered sweet potatoes hold their own vis-à-vis the more pretentious eateries in town. The salad bar (they tried to retire it but regulars squawked) always features

some special delicacy, such as balsamic-doused cherry tomatoes with fresh mozzarella *boccancini* (bite-size pieces)—bravo! Bargain hunters will want to check out the $10 buffet breakfast. *71 Easton St., tel. 508/228–8674. AE, MC, V. No smoking. Closed Mon. and Labor Day–Memorial Day. No lunch. www.pointbreeze.com*

**$$–$$$** **SCHOONERS.** The theme is definitely nautical, but smartly so: flags strung from the rafters and navy awnings over the sidewalk café seem right at home on Steamboat Wharf. The menu is fairly pro forma (rings, wings, steamers, shore dinners), but the pricing is nice, considering what they could get away with. *31 Easy St., tel. 508/228–5824. AE, MC, V. Closed mid-Oct.–Mar. www.spiceoflifeonnantucket.com*

**$$–$$$** **THE TAP ROOM.** Dark and clubby, this basement eatery in the Jared Coffin House (☞ Where to Sleep) looks lifted from John Cheever territory: you'll see people huddled at the bar at all times of day. In summer the restaurant spills onto a flowery patio—a rather more cheerful place to partake of WASPy staples such as baked scrod and prime rib. *29 Broad St., tel. 508/228–2400. AE, D, DC, MC, V. www.jaredcoffinhouse.net*

**$$–$$$** **THE TAVERN.** This is the two-tier restaurant with deck you can't help noticing just off Straight Wharf. Its bar has colonized the bandstand in the middle of the cobblestone square, and the whole place is almost always mobbed—partly thanks to a middle-of-the-road menu that stresses seafood (mostly fried or broiled) and TGIF-type desserts like mud pie. *1 Harbor Sq., tel. 508/228–1266. AE, MC, V. Closed Nov.–Apr.*

**$$–$$$** **VINCENT'S.** One might be tempted to bypass Vincent's because, in this fiercely competitive field, it doesn't look like a real contender. That's precisely its strength. This relaxed restaurant, little changed since 1954, is where islanders go to enjoy a really good meal, freshly prepared, generously portioned, and refreshingly free of pretense. The dishes may not be uniformly cutting-edge, but neither are they retro. The variety is phenomenal: the menu has upwards of three dozen entrées, and not one disappoints. *21 S. Water St., tel. 508/228–0189. MC, V. No smoking. Closed Nov.–Mar.*

**$$ ROSE & CROWN PUB.** Crayon-friendly paper tablecloths and a children's menu cater to a family audience early in the evening; Later, DJs and signature drinks stoke the post-collegiate crowd. There's nothing very special about the menu (who could foresee the day when a goat cheese pizza would seem ordinary?), but you can amuse yourself, while waiting, by studying the old signs hung about this former carriage livery. *23 S. Water St., tel. 508/228–2595. AE, MC, V. Closed Jan.–Mar. www.theroseandcrown.com*

**$$ SUSHI BY YOSHI.** This tiny restaurant enjoys the prodigious output of Yoshihisa Mabuchi, a welcome "washashore" originally from Japan. The sushi and sashimi, available in dozens of guises, are nonpareil: try a special concoction such as the Caterpillar, a veggie roll wrapped in avocado. Also available are classic dishes ranging from *gyoza* (fried pork dumplings) to *udon* (white chunky noodles), *soba* (buckwheat noodles), and teriyaki and, for dessert, green-tea ice cream, bean cakes, and banana tempura. *2 E. Chestnut St., tel. 508/228–1801. No credit cards. No smoking. Closed Nov.–May.*

**$–$$ CAP'N TOBEY'S CHOWDER HOUSE.** A fish house of the old-fashioned sort—lots of wood paneling, nautical mishmash decor—this isn't everyone's cup of bouillabaisse (although it's on the menu here, called "Nantucket Fisherman's Kettle"). If you've missed the likes of seafood au gratin or baked stuffed jumbo shrimp, here's the place to get your '50s fix. *Straight Wharf, tel. 508/228–0836. AE, D, DC, MC, V. Closed mid-Oct.–May.*

**$–$$ FOG ISLAND CAFE.** ★ Cherished year-round for its stellar breakfasts—*Gourmet* requested the recipe for chicken hash—Fog Island is just as fine a spot for lunch or for a most charitably priced dinner. The somewhat small quarters are cheerily decked out in a fresh country style (echoed in the friendly service), and chef-owners Mark and Anne Dawson—both grads of the prestigious Culinary Institute of America—seem determined to provide the best possible value to transients and natives alike. Consider starting the day with, say, pesto scrambled eggs and ending it with Fog-style fajitas. Finally, fine food for the proletariat! *7 S. Water St., tel. 508/228–1818. MC, V. No smoking. www.fogisland.com*

**$–$$ NANTUCKET TAPAS.** Flanking a broad deli case (where you can consider dessert for later) is a cluster of café tables, ideal for noshing à deux, and several sets of barrels topped with broad planks, where a family can comfortably pass and partake. Sharing is definitely the name of the game here, but play with caution: the cost for an assortment of small plates—appetizers, really—can quickly add up. Start with some pork fried dumplings or crab cakes, throw in some tuna carpaccio or Szechuan beef, and boom, you've got a meal. At last: A choose-it-yourself tasting menu for those afraid to commit. *15 S. Beach St., tel. 508/228–2033. MC, V. www.nantuckettapas.com*

**$–$$ WHITE DOG CAFE.** The patio outside the Gaslight Theatre morphs into a delightful little restaurant come summer, serving nicely prepared fish and more amid twining greenery and talk of coming attractions. *1 N. Union St., tel. 508/228–4479. AE, DC, MC, V. Closed Nov.–Apr.*

**$ ★ BROTHERHOOD OF THIEVES.** That line you see snaking down Broad Street? They're would-be patrons of this no-fuss, no-phone, faux-1840s whaling bar. Its history may be pure artifice, but the seasoned curly fries and juicy burgers are insistently, deliciously real. And would you believe it? Folk music lives! *23 Broad St., no phone. No credit cards. No smoking.*

**$ THE FOOD FARE AT THE HARBOR HOUSE.** Who'd figure on one of the island's nicer, bigger inns—one based on a grand hotel built in 1886—being a magnet for the all-you-can-eat crowd? The traditional Sunday brunch buffet in this large, handsome space has proved so popular over the years that it made sense to extend the concept to dinner. A "create your own pasta" station, numerous salad and entrée options, and about a dozen desserts hook the

# island dining

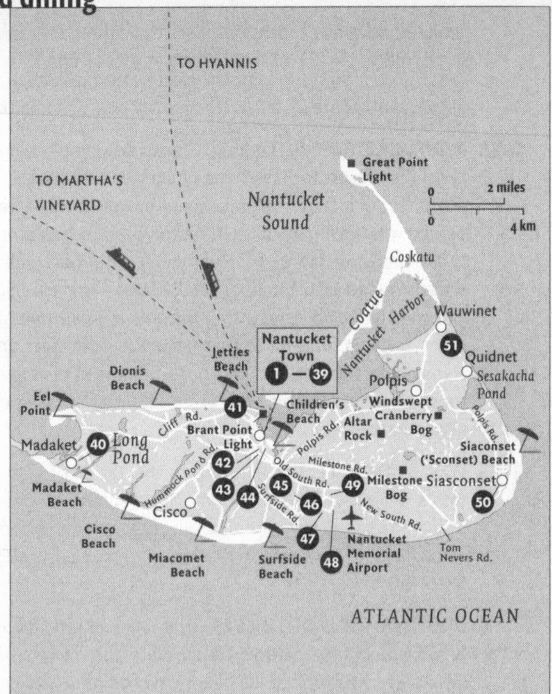

family crowd. A nice touch: kids feast at roughly half-price. *S. Beach St., tel. 508/325–1364. AE, DC, MC, V. No smoking. Closed Jan.–Apr.*

## DINING ELSEWHERE

**$$$$ THE CHANTICLEER.** For more than two decades, chef Jean-Charles Berruet has been wowing Nantucket's elite with classical French cuisine in a *haute auberge* setting in 'Sconset. Don't let the clematis-veiled summerhouse-look deceive you: this is very serious stuff. If you're looking for the ultimate in traditional Gallic finesse (lobster soufflé, perhaps?), you've come to the right place. Three dining rooms surround a lavish garden. Each has an appealing ambience, but the front-runner is clearly the formal room directly opposite the gate. (Given that you're going to shell out several hundred dollars for dinner, you might want to scope out the options ahead of time.) All three rooms enjoy access to the notable, if predictably pricy, 40,000-bottle wine cellar. Lunch is a budget option, relatively speaking, *bien sur. 9 New St., Siasconset, tel. 508/257–6231, www.thechanticleerinn.com. Reservations required. Jacket required. AE, MC, V. No smoking. Closed Mon. and mid-Oct.–early May.*

**$$$$ THE GALLEY.** The only restaurant actually on the beach (the Cliffside Beach Club's private swath), the Galley is awfully fancy for what's essentially a fenced-in tent. The life-size odalisque that occupies the entry is something of a tip-off: expect all-out *luxe, calme, et volupté*, starting with lobster spring rolls, perhaps, followed by roast quail on a brilliant bed of beet risotto. The prices are up there in Nantucket's already lofty stratosphere, but chef James Gee's creations, not to mention the setting, warrant the tariff. *54 Jefferson Ave., tel. 508/228–9641. AE, MC, V. Closed Oct.–May. www.galleynantucket.com*

**$$$$ THE SUMMER HOUSE.** ★ In capturing the essence of 'Sconset, this rose-canopied complex epitomizes Nantucket as well. Flower-laden cottages encircle the lawn and veranda, where you'll want to sip a preprandial cocktail. The interior is abloom as well, with lavish floral displays, all the more resplendent against a background of pastel linen and white wicker. The cuisine is energized, rather than rarefied. All sorts of influences artfully converge in such signature dishes as an entrée combining Szechuan seared tuna, lobster-tail tempura with tangerine soy emulsion, and grapefruit-braised greens. Desserts are equally eclectic, and fabulous. If you had only one night on Nantucket and wanted to be sure it was delightful, this should top your list of destinations. The restaurant also serves lunch by the pool on the beach—a surfeit of pleasures. 17 *Ocean Ave., tel. 508/257–9976. Reservations essential. AE, MC, V. No smoking. Closed mid-Oct.–May. www.spiceoflifeonnantucket.com*

**$$$$** ★ **TOPPER'S.** Poised between the bay and sea, the Wauwinet (☞ Where to Sleep)—an ultraluxuriously restored 19th-century inn on Nantucket's northeastern shore—is where islanders and visitors alike go to experience perfection. Many take advantage of the complimentary launch service aboard the *Wauwinet Lady* from Straight Wharf, which frames the journey with a scenic harbor tour. Having traipsed along the Wauwinet pier and up the croquet lawn (past a life-size sculpted chess set), you'll enter a creamy-white dining room awash with glorious flowers. Chris Freeman's cuisine delivers on the fantasy with a classically inspired menu pumped up with ample creative torque. Seared scallops, for instance, crown a bed of bright-green, basil *brandade* (puree of smoked cod); sautéed lobster arrives atop roe-pinkened fettuccine. Desserts are like childhood dreams brought sophisticatedly up to date. 120 *Wauwinet Rd., tel. 508/228–8768. Reservations essential. Jacket required. AE, DC, MC, V. No smoking. Closed Nov.–Apr. www.wauwinet.com*

**$$$–$$$$** **THE BLACK ANGUS GRILLE.** Done up in hunter green with cranberry-floral accents, this mid-island restaurant—backed by Cioppino's and former staffers—addresses the dedicated carnivores in our midst with sizable slabs of steak (naturally), as well as veal, pork, chicken, fish, and lobster. You will not lack for protein; however, preparation and presentation can be a bit plain, especially at these prices. Fortunately, there appear to be plenty of die-hard nonfoodies hereabouts, willing to pay a premium for prime ingredients in recognizable configurations. *17 Old South Rd., tel. 508/228–9852. D, DC, MC, V. No smoking. Closed Jan.–Mar. No lunch.*

**$$$** **THE SCONSET CAFÉ.** It looks like a modest lunchroom, with chockablock tables virtually within arm's reach of the open kitchen. But this tiny institution, treasured by summering locals since 1983, puts out wonderful breakfasts, great lunches, and outright astounding dinners. The nightly menus shift every two weeks to take advantage of seasonal bounty—vide the piquant plum tomato tart Tatin. And if you can't get in (it's not exactly undiscovered), you can always order out and feast on the beach. *Post Office Sq., Siasconset, tel. 508/257–4008. Reservations essential. No credit cards. BYOB. Closed Oct.–mid-May.*

**$$$** **SEAGRILLE.** Though it may lack the flashy profile of other top island restaurants, this mid-island eatery deserves a place amid the pantheon. Initial impressions are not promising: it's in a bland-looking building plunked next to a gas station. The boxy dining room, softened by hyacinth-print café curtains and murals of wharf and street scenes, is restful, almost subdued, as are the polite, preppy-dressed patrons. Then a dish such as the free-form lobster ravioli shows up, a luscious composition involving shiitake mushrooms, fresh peas, ricotta, and herb beurre blanc, and suddenly you're sitting up and taking notice. The pepita-crusted rack of lamb is a knockout—five ribs' worth, so you'll be forced to take some home (aww), and the truffle cake that is just that, a chocolate truffle big as a cupcake. No wonder chef EJ Harvey and his wife, Robin, who's the friendly maîtresse d', have attracted such a devoted following. *45 Sparks Ave., tel. 508/325–5700. AE, MC, V. No smoking. No lunch. www.theseagrille.com*

**$$$** **WEST CREEK CAFE.** A rehabbed ranch house in the mid-island commercial district would seem to be the last place to seek out cosmopolitan panache, but this hideaway—owned by Pat Tyler of the lamented Second Story, a trendsetter in the '80s—is full of surprises. Purple satin pillows and faux-zebra banquettes snazz up the cool gray barroom; the other two rooms are crackle-painted in a sunny palate, and one has a working fireplace. The menu shifts every two weeks, but you can entrust yourself to chef Jamie Hurley, who has the good sense to pair, say, cornmeal-crusted striped bass with toasted pecan slaw and warm chive potato salad. *11 W. Creek Rd., tel. 508/228–4943. MC, V. No smoking. Closed Tues. No lunch.*

**$$–$$$ CAFE BELLA VITA.** So thoroughly has northern Italian eclipsed the southern staples that it can be a real treat to come upon the classics done right—minestrone; parmigiana; and, of course, pasta in all its less-trendy guises. Though small and plunked in a rather bland mid-island mall, this engaging little trattoria boasts plenty of brio, and some killer garlic-intensive grilled scampi. *Bayberry Court, tel. 508/228–8766. MC, V. No smoking. Closed Mon.*

**$$–$$$ SFOGLIA.** Young chefs Ron and Colleen Suhanosky enjoy a marriage made in culinary school (the top-ranked Culinary Institute of America) and enhanced by stints at stellar restaurants and homestays in rural Italy. Sfoglia debuted in the summer of '00, a celery-tinted trattoria with mismatched tables (including some enamel-top honeys from the '40s), chairs, crockery, even silverware. The effect is charming, and almost perversely stylish. The menu features such homey dishes as fluffy gnocchi with pesto, ziti tossed with spiced eggplant and braised lamb, and roasted whole *branzino* (a troutlike Mediterranean fish) infused with wild fennel. Desserts—Colleen's province—include an ultrasilky *panna cotta* (chilled egg custard flavored with caramel). *130 Pleasant St., tel. 508/325–4500. No credit cards. No smoking.*

**$$–$$$ THE WESTENDER.** Downstairs, in the bar, a youngish set quaffs "Madaket Mysteries" (the none-too-secret ingredient is dark rum) and nibbles on barbecue roll-ups and other café fare. Upstairs, in a cathedral-ceiling space with optimal sunset-over-the-water views, the menu is more ambitious: pan-roasted trout with almond-pistachio butter and rock-shrimp risotto as well as grilled salmon with mango pepper relish and conch potato cakes. Madaket is no longer the sleepy little outpost that it once was. Expect a mob. *326 Madaket Rd., tel. 508/228–5100. AE, D, MC, V. No smoking. Closed Nov.–Apr. www.spiceoflifeonnantucket.com*

**$$–$$$ WINDSONG.** To be honest, it's hard to muster the highest of hopes for the rather corporate-looking dining room at the Nantucket Inn (☞ Where to Stay), a distinctly un-innlike spread next to the Nantucket Airport. But the traditionally appointed space—the size of a small hangar—is pleasantly comfy, and local chef Bruce Yancy dishes up the best lobster preparation (as in tender morsels tossed with asparagus and penne) encountered over many an evening of rigorous research. So, if your plane's fogged in, don't despair; instead, repair here for a compensatory repast. *27 Macy's La., tel. 508/228–6900. AE, D, DC, MC, V. No smoking. Closed Nov.–Mar.*

**$$ A.K. DIAMOND'S.** Steaks and seafoods rule at this spacious, clubby cousin of Arno's (☞ *above*), close to the airport. Natives flock here to take advantage of the early-bird discounts (of 25%–50%) and to bulk up at the salad bar. Expect cravings for the hefty slabs of cranberry-barbecue ribs to inspire another visit. *16 Macy's La., tel. 508/228–3154. AE, D, DC, MC, V. No smoking. www.akdiamonds.net*

**$$ THE PIZZA JOINT.** A smattering of tables painted in primary colors and no fewer than 53 optional toppings are what elevates this eatery from its own somewhat derogatory tag. An elegant night out? Hardly. A satisfying one? Of that you can be sure. *7 Daves St., tel. 508/325–4385. AE, MC, V. No smoking.*

**$–$$ BAMBOO SUPPER CLUB.** More bar than restaurant, and commensurately rowdy, this mid-island watering hole does serve a not-so-light menu—from baked Brie to New York strip steak—

at prices that maintain a faithful local following. *3 Chin's Way, tel. 508/228–0200. AE, MC, V.*

**$–$$ FAREGROUNDS.** Buffalo wings, potato skins, jalapeño poppers—you know the drill. Set mid-island, Faregrounds—along with its smoking-allowed adjunct, Pudley's Pub—offers the type of something-for-everyone menu now found at middle-brow restaurants across America: munchies, pizza, steaks, seafood, and the de rigueur salad bar. You might find it all a bit boring, and the din deafening—the place is that popular—but the prices sure are welcoming. *27 Faregrounds Rd., tel. 508/228–4095. AE, D, DC, MC, V. www.faregrounds.com*

**$–$$ THE HEN HOUSE.** Another mid-island destination for the non-trust-funded, this unassuming restaurant started out as a breakfast joint catering to the island's large Irish summer work-force—you can still get bangers with your eggs—and soon turned into a source of three square meals, mostly of the stick-to-your-ribs school (baby-back ribs, rib-eye steak, etc.). The menu hints at higher aspirations, but for a few dollars more you could score more ambience in town. *1 Chin's Way, tel. 508/228–2639. No credit cards.*

**$ HUTCH'S.** Nantucket's airport is almost as cute as the one depicted on the defunct TV show *Wings*, only a bit bigger. The same goes for its restaurant, open for three meals—and not just burgers but all sorts of blue-plate specials—year-round. "Jamaican night," on summer Wednesdays, attracts the seasonal workforce, as well as resident spice-cravers. *Nantucket Memorial Airport, tel. 508/228–5550. D.*

## PREPARED FOOD SHOPS

Having a spontaneous picnic? These purveyors, with the goods to go, are a step ahead of you. No seating is available, although some have outdoor benches.

**Bartlett's Ocean View Farm** (Bartlett Farm Rd., tel. 508/228–9403) has fabulous island-grown produce, plus superb main dishes, salads, baked goods, and desserts.

The **Complete Kitchen** (25 Centre St., tel. 508/257–2665) mostly sells cooking gear but has some foodstuffs and a sandwich counter.

**Cook's Cafe** (6 South Beach St., tel. 508/228–8810) has smoothies, wraps, and rice bowls to go.

**Damiano's** (14 Amelia Dr., tel. 508/228–5879) is an Italian grocery with hand-cut meats, homemade pastas, and prepared dishes.

**Fahey & Fromagerie** (49A Pleasant St., tel. 508/325–5644) has something for even the most finicky of epicures, from goat cheese tartlets to roasted free-range chickens, plus all sorts of packaged delicacies and an outstanding wine selection.

**Fast Forward** (117 Orange St., tel. 508/228–5807) is Espresso's (☞ *above*) edge-of-town satellite, which offers the same coffees, sandwiches, and pastries.

**Joe's Broad Street Grill** (10 Broad St., tel. 508/228–4746) has sandwiches, subs, burgers, and even some vegetarian alternatives.

The **Juice Bar & Bakery** (12 Broad St., tel. 508/228–5799) is home of the absolutely best ice cream—spring for a waffle cone and homemade hot fudge—plus pastries and, oh yes, fresh juices.

**Juice Guys** (4 Easy St., tel. 508/228–4464) is a cheerful storefront where you can stock up on Nantucket Nectars and sample special blends.

**Maine Coffee Roasters** (4 Broad St., tel. 800/228–2224, www.nantucketcoffee.com) has the freshest beans plus assorted pastries, including some decadent cookies.

## Quick Cranberry Chronology

*Native Americans called them "bitter berries" and used them as a dye, a poultice, and as food, typically sweetened with maple sap (they were probably still pretty sour). Dutch settlers called them* kraanbere, *noting a resemblance between the creeping vine's pale pink flowers and the head and beak of a crane (it's a bit of a stretch).*

*Massachusetts calls them a cash crop—or did, until the 2000 season, when a surfeit sent prices plummeting. Environmentalists still call them a godsend, because cranberry bogs under cultivation require a broad protective border of wildlife-friendly wetlands, which would otherwise be subject to the pressures of development.*

*Let's just call them delicious—along with other New England delicacies, such as lobster, which colonists initially spurned as pig fodder and prisoners protested against well into the 19th century. Though cranberries have yet to penetrate markets abroad (one reason for the current glut), they've found their way into regional recipes. Nantucket Nectars mades a popular cranberry lemonade and Sweet Inspirations (☞ Shopping) ships its chocolate-covered cranberries to appreciative clients around the world.*

**Nantucket Bagel Company** (5 W. Creek Rd., tel. 508/228–6461) bakes bagels on site and also serves muffins, wraps, and specialty sandwiches.

The **Nantucket Bake Shop** (79 Orange St., tel. 508/228–2797 or 800/440–2253, www.nantucketbakeshop.com) has "savories," which include a dozen or so varieties of croissants and quiche. Best of the sweets? The lemon poppyseed cake.

**Nantucket Gourmet** (4 India St., tel. 508/228–4353) has all the necessary kitchen paraphernalia, plus ready-to-eat delicacies, from cheeses to pâtés, plus one delicious daily soup and sandwich.

**Sayle's Seafood** (99 Washington St. Ext., tel. 508/228–4599) serves plenty of fresh fish, plus lobster dinners and more to go, plus clambakes wherever you wish.

**Souza's Seafood** (23 Trotter's La., tel. 508/228–9140) has fresh seafood of all sorts, homemade chowder, smoked scallops, and lobster travel packs.

**Stars** (Straight Wharf, tel. 508/228–1095) is strictly for sweets, from ice cream and frozen yogurt to fudge.

**Steamboat Pizza** (10 Broad St., tel. 508/228–1131) is nothing special, but it's available till 2 AM.

**Stubby's** (Steamboat Wharf, no phone) is known for trendy fast food, from "Mini Me" burgers to Cuban sandwiches.

**Tacos Tacos** (10 Broad St., tel. 508/228–5418) serves up what is obviously junk—just check out the cans stacked behind the counter—but the nachos are, oh, so satisfying.

## LIGHT FARE

At these quicky, inexpensive eateries, without real table service, you'll be seated either at a counter or at one of a few informal tables.

**$ CLAUDETTE'S.** For a great picnic in 'Sconset, stop here for a box lunch to go; or dig right in on the shady patio. *Post Office Sq., 'Sconset, tel. 508/257–6622. No credit cards. Closed mid-Oct.–mid-May. No dinner.*

**$ DAILY BREADS BAKERY.** Foccaccia sandwiches and hearty pastries are yours to eat on-site or to carry off. *147 Orange St., tel. 508/228–8961. No credit cards. No smoking.*

**$ DAVID'S SODA FOUNTAIN.** David Skokan dispenses the blueberry muffins, sandwiches, ice cream, and wry wit at old-fashioned Congdon's Pharmacy. *47 Main St., tel. 508/228–4549. No credit cards. No smoking.*

**$ THE DOWNYFLAKE.** Bountiful breakfasts—featuring homemade doughnuts—and well-priced lunches. *18 Sparks Ave., tel. 508/228–4533. No credit cards. No smoking. No dinner.*

**$ ESPRESSO CAFE.** This former ice cream parlor, with its tin ceilings and harlequin-tile floor, is no mere restaurant but is the very heart of town—especially off-season. Any time of year, it's the first place to head for a fancy coffee, pastry binge, or creative meal. In summer you can schlep your tray to the shady patio out back, an oasis that visitors don't always discover. *40 Main St., tel. 508/228–6930. D, MC, V. No smoking. Open year-round.*

**$ HENRY'S.** Henry's serves sandwiches, grinders, and roll-ups to order and has since the mid-'70s. *2 Broad St., tel. 508/228–0123. No credit cards. No smoking. Closed Nov.–Apr.*

**$ HENRY'S JR.** This is Henry's (☞ *above*) inland offshoot, with the same sandwiches and fare—open year-round. *129 Orange St., tel. 508/228–3035, No credit cards. No smoking.*

**$ THE JETTIES.** More than a mere beach concession stand, the Jetties has good fast food and ample shaded seating; it's available for private parties at night. *Jetties Beach, tel. 508/325–6347. MC, V. Closed Labor Day–Memorial Day.*

**$ MAC'S PLACE.** A family idyll at Children's Beach: youngsters get to clamber all over the playground while awaiting terrific breakfasts (peach pancakes!) and yummy lunches. The homemade doughnuts get scarfed fresh out of the oven. *Off Harbor Way at Children's Beach, tel. 508/228–3127. No credit cards. No smoking. Closed Oct.–mid-May. No dinner.*

**$ MUSE PIZZA.** Here you'll find all the usual bar munchies, plus sandwiches, subs, and a dozen pizzas. Bonus: they'll deliver to the beach. *44 Surfside Rd., tel. 508/228–1471. No credit cards.*

**$ NANTUCKET BEACH WOK.** Come here for stir-fries in every imaginable combination, including the Chinese standards. 1

## Divine Picnic Spots

*Picnic ops crop up the minute you step off the boat. Virtually all the town sidewalks are lined with inviting benches (businesses apparently compete for whose is the cutest), and lots of visitors graze as they stroll. Special sanctuaries, which first-timers may not know about, include the beautiful garden of the Atheneum (entrance on India Street), with its blossoming trees tough enough for clambering children; Children's Beach, where youngsters can really stretch their legs and more on a well-equipped playground; and Lily Pond, off North Liberty Street, which is actually a fresh-water marsh with great appeal for birds—and birders.*

*Out of town, there's no end to the possibilities—or, for that matter, the beaches. Inland, Altar Rock—the island's high spot off Polpis Road midway to 'Sconset—offers the most sweeping views, relatively speaking, although the picnic tables plunked right next to the Bartlett Farm greenhouse, source of stellar produce and ready-to-eat treats, are a definite favorite.*

*Toombs Court, on Old South Rd., tel. 508/325–9999. AE, D, MC, V. Closed Nov.–Dec.*

**$ PROVISIONS.** Superb soups and sandwiches are the lure here, including the muffaletta (a salami-provolone hero with olive tapenade) and "Turkey Terrific" (Thanksgiving to go). *3 Harbor Sq., tel. 508/228–3258. No credit cards. No smoking. Closed Jan.–Mar. No dinner.*

**$ THE ROTARY.** Here, beside the endless stream of traffic, is where the non-trust-funders chow down, at normal-people prices. The homemade breakfasts are bountiful. *Milestone Rotary, tel. 508/228–9505. MC, V. No smoking. Closed Sun. and late Dec.–mid-Mar. No dinner.*

**$ THE SHACK.** Right on the bike path, halfway to Surfside Beach, the Shack—a real one—beckons the hungry with "Shark Attack" burgers, supersize lobster rolls, milk shakes, and more. *63 Surfside Rd., tel. 508/228–6690. No credit cards.*

**$ THE SODA FOUNTAIN.** The Nantucket Pharmacy has a more '50s-modern look than Congdon's, plus unbeatable lobster rolls. *45 Main St., tel. 508/228–0180. No credit cards. No smoking.*

**$ SOMETHING NATURAL.** A pleasant stroll (or bike ride) up Cliff Road, this rustic bakery also serves up savory sandwiches. *50 Cliff Rd., tel. 508/228–0504. No credit cards. No smoking. Closed Nov.–Mar. No dinner.*

**$ SOMETHING NATURAL DOWNTOWN.** The "downtown" bit is meant to be ironic, but the excellent sandwiches are quite sincere. *6 Oak St., tel. 508/325–7838. No credit cards. No smoking. Closed Nov.–Apr.*

**$ SURFSIDE SUBS.** You can grab gourmet sandwiches on French bread here, en route to Surfside Beach. *1 Windy Way, tel. 508/325–0060. No credit cards. Closed Oct.–Apr.*

## MARKETS IN NANTUCKET TOWN

**Ack Natural** (95 Washington St. Ext., tel. 508/228–4554, www.acknatural.com) has organic staples, including some fresh produce.

**A & P** (Salem St., at Straight Wharf, tel. 508/228–9756) is serviceable, albeit a bit cramped and grubby, with good produce.

**Allserve General Store** (Straight Wharf, tel. 508/228–8170) sells basics for the boat basin—and is the birthplace of Nantucket Nectars.

**Cumberland Farms** (115 Orange St., tel. 508/228–7071) is a charmless quickie-mart.

**Nantucket Natural** (29 Centre St., tel. 508/228–3947) has natural foods, mostly prepackaged, and a juice bar.

**Straight Wharf Fish Store** (Harbor Sq., Straight Wharf, tel. 508/228–1095) sells slabs straight from the sea.

## MARKETS ELSEWHERE

**East Coast Seafood** (167 Hummock Pond Rd., tel. 508/228–2871) is a seafood shop conveniently near Bartlett's Farm.

**Glidden's Island Sea Food** (115 Pleasant St., tel. 508/228–0912) has been selling mostly fish and shellfish since 1898. It also has lobster to go.

**Moors End Farm** (401 Polpis Rd., tel. 508/228–2674) has fresh produce in season.

**Old South Market** (57 Old South Rd., tel. 508/228–9677) is your basic mini-mart.

**Sconset Market** (Post Office Sq., tel. 508/257–9915) is a seasonal shop with fresh foods and gourmet necessities.

**Stop & Shop** (129 Pleasant St., tel. 508/228–2178) is as large and well stocked as its mainland counterparts, with comparable pricing.

**Westender Market** (326 Madaket Rd., tel. 508/228–5100) sells staples for this growing village.

*The power shopper emerges from the dark lower deck of the Hy-Line ferry. She totes a straw bag stocked with the tools of her trade: credit cards, cash, shopping list, Fodor's guide, and a change of shoes. Her plan is to begin at Lower Main Street and work from there. As she pauses to view the numerous shops before her and the others she knows lurk just out of sight on side streets, she realizes this may be the challenge of her life: so many shops, so little time.*

## In This Chapter



*Revised and updated by Joyce Wagner*

# shopping

**EVER SINCE SEA CAPTAINS** in the early 1800s brought merchandise back from their excursions to foreign ports of call and restless sailors wove lightship baskets to pass the long hours aboard ship, Nantucket has enjoyed an active shopping scene. Today Nantucket Town has a decidedly modern shopping district, with more decorative home furnishing stores, high-quality art galleries, and high-end clothing boutiques filling the *très cher* retail space. These boutiques certainly balance out the town's omnipresent T-shirt shops and offer a fashion rejoinder to the all-cotton outfits comprised of Nantucket reds—pants, hats, you name it, which fade to a salmon shade of pink with washing. Despite its expensive taste, Nantucket is foremost a casual place: Even the high-powered who frequent in summer can be spotted in a comfy pair of flip-flops. You should do the same.

## When and How

Most of Nantucket's shops are seasonal, opening sometime after April and closing between Labor Day and November, though a few stay open longer for the year-rounders.

### SHOPPING SPOTS

Nantucket Town's commercial district is bounded by the waterfront and Main, Broad, and Centre streets, continuing along South Beach Street. Old South Wharf, built in 1770, has distinctive crafts, clothing, and antiques stores; a ship's chandlery; and art galleries in small, shedlike structures that, from the outside, look more like boathouses than shops. Straight Wharf, where the Hy-Line ferry docks, has T-shirt and other tourist-oriented shops, a gallery, a museum, and restaurants. Phones and rest rooms are at the end of the wharf. The few shops in outlying areas are generally service-oriented (food stores, hardware, etc.).

## SPECIALTY SHOPS

### ANTIQUES

Step into another time in the wood-fragrant shop of **Charles Spada** (2 Quince St. behind Centre St., tel. 508 /325–0501). It carries lots of French and American primitive wooden furniture, and manager Patricia Kastner is more than willing to explain some of the more obscure pieces, such as the 19th-century pewter meat platter that uses hot water to keep the entrée warm.

**Fleur-de-Lis** (27 Easy St., tel. 508/325–0700) stocks lots of shabby chic furniture (dressers, side tables, bookshelves, breakfronts, etc.) from the 1920s to the 1940s and other home furnishings that won't break the bank. Owner Sue Drabkin also designs and sells her own jewelry line, probably the only non-Nantucket-theme jewelry on the island.

**Forager House Collection** (20 Centre St., tel. 508/228–5977) specializes in folk art and Americana, including whirligigs, vintage postcards, lightship baskets, antique maps, charts, and prints, and a nice selection of vintage quilts.

**Island Antiques** (5 Miacomet Ave., tel. 508/325–5852), with its auctioneer and appraiser, Mark J. Enik, acquires most of its inventory from fine Nantucket estates and holds auctions frequently during the summer. Watch for dates in the local papers.

Climb the wide stairs lined with tolework-decorated wastebaskets and other home accessories to **Janis Aldridge** (50 Main St., tel. 508/228–6673) for beautifully framed antique engravings,

## Auctions

*If you've never been to an auction, check the local papers, grab your checkbook, and jump right in. Nantucket in the summer is a mecca for auction aficionados, with a few regular, commercial auctioneers like Rafael Osona, Mark J. Enik, and McLaughlin & Associates hosting events. Whether silent or traditional, auctions are a fun and unique opportunity to purchase one-of-a-kind items, often at a bargain. In fact, many island charities raise much of their yearly income this way. Although the poor stooge who inadvertently purchases a pricey Picasso by scratching his nose is pretty much the fantasy of sitcom writers, you should ask questions at the door. Even if you've no intention of purchasing anything, it's a sure bet you'll change your mind in the heat of the bidding. Be prepared to be overwhelmed.*

including architectural and botanical prints, home furnishings, and contemporary art.

**Leonards** (31 Washington St., tel. 508/228–0620) sells fine antique and reproduction furniture with a special emphasis on heirloom quality beds. Pieces are constructed with quality in mind—hand-scraping is used instead of sanding to bring out the brilliance and texture of the wood—and items are priced accordingly.

**Manor House Antiques** (31½ Centre St., tel. 508/228–4335) is not easy to find but worth the effort. Brightly lit cases display the glass, porcelain, and silver collections of 10 dealers.

**Nina Hellman Antiques** (48 Centre St., tel. 508/228–4677) carries scrimshaw, whaling artifacts, ship models, nautical instruments, and other marine antiques, plus folk art and Nantucket memorabilia. Charles Manghis, a contemporary scrimshaw artist, demonstrates and exhibits his craft here.

**Rafael Osona** (American Legion Hall, 21 Washington St., tel. 508/228–3942; for a schedule, write to Box 2607, 02584) holds auctions of fine antiques from Memorial Day to early December. Items include 18th- through 20th-century American, English, and Continental furniture, decorative accessories, and art.

**Tonkin of Nantucket** (33 Main St., tel. 508/228–9697) has two floors of fine English antiques—including furniture, china, art, silver, scientific instruments, and Staffordshire miniatures—as well as new sailors' valentines and lightship baskets.

**Wayne Pratt** (28 Main St., tel. 508/228–8788) specializes in American antiques and handcrafted reproductions. Pieces include baskets, leather-top desks and tables, and many maritime antiques.

## ART GALLERIES

**Cavalier Galleries** (7 Salem St., tel. 508/325–4405) is a sculpture lover's dream. Life-size bronzes of children at play decorate the entranceway garden, and diminutive to larger-than-life works are plentiful inside, as are fine-art paintings, prints, and photographs.

The collection of studio glass at **Dane Gallery** (28 Centre St., tel. 508/228–7779) is extensive and justifiably expensive. The brilliantly colored glass sculptures of Dale Chihuly and the fanciful "Tutti Frutti" goblets by Robert Dane are well worth seeing.

**Gallery on Centre** (32 Centre St., tel. 508/228–9977) showcases contemporary artwork from all over the country. You can't miss the oversize Robert Bery photographs in thick brushed-metal frames. Featured artists change weekly in the summer.

The **Gallery on Four India** (4 India St., tel. 508/228–8509) is a quiet, spacious refuge, with high-end 19th-century American and marine paintings.

**Lannan Ship Model Gallery** (12 Oak St., tel. 508/325–7797) is a shop with the feel of a museum where you can see the graceful sailing vessels of bygone days in miniature. The models are painstakingly handcrafted and intricately rigged.

**Robert Wilson Galleries** (34 Main St., tel. 508/228–2096) carries high-end, fine-art versions of Nantucket scenes, plus outstanding contemporary American marine, impressionist, and other art.

Be sure to include **Sailors' Valentine Gallery, Salon and Sculpture Garden** (Macy's Warehouse, Lower Main St., tel. 508/228–2011) on your short list to see the island's most interesting collection of contemporary fine and folk art, sculpture, and exquisite sailors' valentines.

## BOOKS

Look for the Nantucket Room at **Mitchell's Book Corner** (54 Main St., tel. 508/228–1080) for all you could want to know about the island and whaling. Many ocean-related children's books plus a cursory sampling of the usual bookstore fare are stocked. Authors appear weekly in summer.

Charming **Nantucket Bookworks** (25 Broad St., tel. 508/228–4000) carries an extensive assortment of hardcover and paperback books, with an emphasis on literary works and Nantucket-specific titles, as well as a children's books and a great assortment of greeting cards.

## CANDY

The smell of chocolate confections cooking in the backroom of **Sweet Inspirations** (26 Centre St., tel. 508/228–5814) will immediately tempt you away from the wholesome diet you're following. Cranberries also appear in various savory forms; dried cranberries, chocolate-covered cranberries, and cranberry honey are favorite examples.

## CLOTHING

**Beautiful People** (13 Centre St., tel. 508/228–2001) lives up to the promise on the sign at its entry: "Styles as diverse as the people who wear them." Fashions range from the casual to the dressy and are available at reasonable prices. The young staff is very courteous and helpful.

**Best & Co.** (40 Centre St., tel. 508/228–8073) sells clothes from infants to size 12, prams, linens, towels, and furniture to flush folks. Look for high-quality dresses with clever smocking, and expect friendly, personal service.

**Cashmere Nantucket** (32 Centre St., tel. 508/228–7611) carries original designs in lush cashmere and rustling taffeta and lots of diaphanous and beaded clothes. These gorgeous articles are very pricey, and the service can be kind of snooty.

Watch your head as you step down into **Cordillera Imports** (18 Broad St., tel. 508/228–6140) for affordable casual clothing and jewelry for young men and women. Sandals, accessories, and crafts from Latin America, Asia, and elsewhere are also stocked.

**Eye of the Needle** (14 Federal St., tel. 508/228–1923) caters to the fabulously dressed—selections are always reminiscent of whatever colorful things they're wearing in Boston, where the store's based—and perhaps the fabulously wealthy: Michael Stars Ts are at the low end, and select pieces from Tocca and Sigerson Morrison shoes are at the other wallet-emptying end.

**Joan Vass** (23 Centre St., tel. 508/228–7118) carries a small stock of sophisticated designs for women in lush fabrics at reasonable prices. The shop's request that cell-phone conversations be held outside guarantees quiet, peaceful shopping.

**Murray's Toggery Shop** (62 Main St., tel. 508/228–0437) sells the famous pants, Nantucket reds—for men, women, and children—and all the other New England standards year-round: chinos, turtlenecks, polos, Birkenstocks, and Timberlands.

**Murray's Warehouse** (7 New St., tel. 508/228–3584) has discounts of up to 50% on items sold in Murray's Toggery Shop (☞ *above*).

**Nantucket Looms** (16 Main St., tel. 508/228–1908) allows customers to watch weavers hand-fashioning sweaters, scarves, throws, and other items at two large wooden looms. The shop is open year-round and also carries distinctive furnishings for home and garden.

**Peach Trees** (19 Main St., tel. 508/228–8555) sells an eclectic, international mix of cleverly designed women's and children's clothes, such as colorful Icelandic sweaters with cityscapes or geometrical patterns; green ice, butterscotch, and mahogany amber jewelry; and a rainbow of shawls from Portugal.

The **Peanut Gallery** (8 India St., off Centre St., tel. 508/228–2010) has a real feeling for real kids. Shop for sweaters, sleepwear, toys, and beachwear with recognizable labels and island-made items. Information about baby-sitters and kids' activities is posted near the door.

At **Vanessa Noel** (1 Orange St., tel. 508/228–6030) you'll fall so in love with the shoes that you'll wish you had two extra feet. They're a bit pricey, but who cares when they look like this?

The inviting windows of **Vis-a-Vis** (34 Main St., tel. 508/228–5527) display unique, funky, and classic women's and children's clothing and accessories. Decorative objects, including hooked rugs, quilts, and collectibles, are also for sale.

**Wolfhound Imports** (21 Main St., tel. 508/228–3552) is a great place to pick up a baby gift. The first floor has European and domestic styles in natural fibers for men and women, and upstairs are the sale, infants', and children's sections.

**Zero Main** (0 Main St., tel. 508/228–4401) has stylish (without being too trendy), casual, and affordably priced women's clothes, including a good selection of (mostly Franco Sarto) shoes.

## CRAFTS

**Claire Murray** (11 S. Water St., tel. 508/228–1913 or 800/252–4733) carries the designer's Nantucket-theme and other hand-hooked rugs and rug kits, quilts, and knitting and needlework kits.

**Erica Wilson Needle Works** (25 Main St., tel. 508/228–9881) sells everything for embroidery and needlepoint, including the famed designer's kits. Look also for decorative items for the home, clothing, hats and accessories, and handmade Nantucket knot jewelry by Heidi Weddendorf.

**Four Winds Craft Guild** (6 Ray's Ct., tel. 508/228–9623) carries a large selection of antique and new scrimshaw and lightship baskets, as well as ship models, duck decoys, and a kit for making your own lightship basket.

**Scrimshander Gallery** (19 Old South Wharf, tel. 508/228–1004) deals in new and antique scrimshaw.

## FARM STANDS

Monday through Saturday in season, colorful farm stands are set up on Main Street to sell local produce and flowers.

At **Bartlett's Ocean View Farm & Greenhouses** (Bartlett Farm Rd. off Hummock Pond Rd., tel. 508/228–9403), a 100-acre farm run by eighth-generation Bartletts, a farm stand is open in season. In June you can pick your own strawberries.

**Moors End Farm** (Polpis Rd., tel. 508/228–2674) is a great source for fresh vegetables, herbs, and cut flowers.

## GIFT SHOPS

Fanciful windows lure you in to **Anderson's of Nantucket** (29 Main St., tel. 508/228–4187), a wonderland of laces, crystal, ceramics, mirrors, and hats. Stop here on the way to that wedding.

**Craftmasters of Nantucket** (7 India St., tel. 508/228–0322) carries posh versions of the typical Nantucket wares—

## Lightship Baskets

Nantucket's signature lightship baskets were first created in the 1820s by Nantucket sailors. These woven rattan baskets with wooden bottoms mimicked the construction of wooden barrels and casks made on Nantucket for the whaling industry, which were based on a round wooden circle or oval, with woven rattan bodies, and lid often ornamented with scrimshaw depicting marine-related scenes. It was not until 1856, when basket molds were brought aboard the South Shoal Lightship, that they were dubbed "lightship baskets." The sailors on the lightships spent nine-month stretches aboard ship, their sole responsibility to warn passing vessels of the treacherous shoals around Sankaty Head. Frequently, there was not much to do. The weaving of baskets was well suited to such a constrained lifestyle, plus it was a time-consuming activity, and the necessary materials were easily obtained during on-shore leave.

Now, the 90 or so members of the Nantucket Lightship Basket Makers Merchants Association ensure the authenticity of their baskets. Products made by these members come with a certificate with the maker's name and location on it. Fake baskets made in Japan or Hong Kong are easily spotted, as many have a loose weave; cane, rather than oak, handles; square, instead of rounded, edges on top and bottom; and stamped, rather than carved, scrimshaw for decoration.

The baskets are now used as purses by those who can afford them—prices range from $300 for new baskets to well over $3,000 for vintage ones. Miniature jewelry versions of the baskets are made by plaiting fine threads of gold or silver wire. Prices start at around $300 for gold versions.

scrimshaw, lightship basket jewelry enhanced with diamonds, saphires, and rubies; and stuffed animals made of mink.

**Museum Shop** (11 Broad St., next to the Whaling Museum, tel. 508/228–5785) has island-related books; antique whaling tools; reproduction furniture; and toys, including reproduction 18th- and 19th-century whirligigs.

**Nantucket Sleigh Ride** (3 India St., tel. 508/325-4980) is the exclusive island distributor for Christopher Radko's collectible blown-glass ornaments.

If heaven had a gift shop, it would look like **Rosa Rugosa** (10 Straight Wharf, tel. 508/228–5597). Roses and other flowers are painted abundantly on the furniture and other items for the home.

**Seven Seas Gifts** (46 Centre St., tel. 508/228–0958) stocks all kinds of inexpensive gift and souvenir items, including shells, baskets, toys, and Nantucket jigsaw puzzles. Captain Pollard, one of a handful of survivors of *The Essex*, lived out his final years a tormented man in this cranberry-color house.

The **Spectrum** (26 Main St., tel. 508/228–4606) sells distinctive art, glass objects, wood boxes, jewelry, and kaleidoscopes.

## HOME FURNISHINGS

At the **Complete Kitchen** (25 Centre St., tel. 508/228–2665) you'll find everything you need to furnish a kitchen worthy of a cooking-show studio, including the food. A refrigerator case is stocked with an extensive line of exotic cheeses and prepared food, or have the staff whip you up a great sandwich at the back counter.

**Devonshire** (35 Centre St., tel. 508/325–8989), "the English garden shop," carries beautiful hand-painted toile-patterned and decoupage-finished tables and dressers, plus pillows, prints, and architectural relics (columns, ironwork, or bas-relief) from demolished vintage buildings.

**Expressions of Dan Freedman** (7 Old South Wharf, tel. 508/228–3291) is the purveyor of the Nantucket Beach Bag Blanket, a cleverly designed picnic or beach blanket that folds up into its own carrying sack. It comes in two sizes.

**Nantucket Gourmet** (4 India St., tel. 508/228–4353) offers the modern kitchen everything from coffeemakers to the famous Nantucket Peppergun, a fast-loading, large capacity, quick-on-the-draw peppermill created and manufactured on the island, which is displayed here on vintage stoves. Check out a complete stock of island foodstuffs on a table near the door.

## JEWELRY

The lightship-basket jewelry at **Diana Kim England Goldsmiths** (56 Main St., tel. 508/228–3766) is named after 'Sconset cottages and is designed and made on the premises. The shop specializes in blue, green, or pink tourmaline; blue-gray chalcedony; and blue tanzanite—unusual gems that are then mounted in rings and necklaces.

**Golden Basket** (44 Main St., tel. 508/228–4344) sells miniature gold and silver lightship baskets, pieces with starfish and shell motifs, and other fine jewelry.

**Golden Nugget** (Straight Wharf, tel. 508/228–1019) is a branch of the Golden Basket (☞ *above*) and stocks similar Nantucket-inspired jewelry and merchandise.

**Jewelers' Gallery of Nantucket** (21 Centre St., tel. 508/228–0229) is the oldest established jewelry store on Nantucket. You'll find jewelry reproductions of lightship baskets, sailors' valentines, as well as estate and contemporary jewelry, and a friendly staff behind the counter.

**Pageo Jewelers** (22 Centre St., tel. 508/228–6899) sells high-end jewelry from all over the world. The inventory includes many large and clunky pieces, but you'll also find some that are intricate and delicate.

## LIQUOR STORES

With about 1,500 varieties, **Island Spirits** (10 Washington St., tel. 508/228–4484) has Nantucket's largest wine selection, but the store also stocks premium liquor, microbrews, and regular beer. It's open year-round Monday–Saturday 8 AM–11 PM mid-May to Columbus Day and 11 AM to 9 PM Columbus Day to mid-May. Delivery is free with a minimum purchase.

**Fahey & Fromagerie** (49A Pleasant St., tel. 508/325–5644) has frequent wine tastings and carries a large selection of wine and beer as well as gourmet cheeses and prepared foods. It's open Monday–Thursday 9–7 and Friday and Saturday 10–8 from April to November.

**Murray's Beverage Store** (23 Main St., tel. 508/228–0071) is a large, busy store in the shopping district, with beer, liquor, and an extensive collection of wines and cigars. Murray's will gladly assemble and deliver (on-island) a gift basket of wines and cheeses. It's open year-round Monday–Saturday 9–11 May–September and 9–7 October–April. Delivery is free.

## NECESSITIES

Ceiling fans and wood paneling lend the **Hub** (31 Main St., tel. 508/228–3868), a vintage kind of feeling. Here you'll find on- and off-island newspapers, books, a wall filled with magazines, and lots of notions and sundries.

## PETS

**Cold Noses** (Straight Wharf, in the Courtyard, tel. 508/228–5477) has everything for Fido and Fluffy, including a sweatshirt for pooches that says, "I *am* the dog from Nantucket."

## PHARMACIES

**Congdon's** (47 Main St., tel. 508/228–0020) is open nightly until 10 from mid-June to mid-September, until 6 in the off-season.

**Island Pharmacy** (122 Pleasant St., tel. 508/228–6400) is open Monday–Saturday year-round until 8, Sunday till 6.

**Nantucket Pharmacy** (45 Main St., tel. 508/228–0180) stays open until 10:30 nightly from Memorial Day to Labor Day and until 6 in the off-season.

## SPORTING GOODS

**Force 5 Watersports** (6 Union St., tel. 508/228–0700) sells skins, boards, and all the paraphernalia and clothing you'll need to go with them, plus a terrific assortment of sandals and bathing suits for merely laying out; it's closed Christman Eve through March.

## TOYS

The **Nantucket Kiteman** (14 S. Water St., tel. 508/228–7089) sells, assembles, and repairs kites for flying at local beaches.

Carrying plenty of its namesake items in various sizes and shapes, **Toy Boat** (41 Straight Wharf, tel. 508/228–4552) also sells other quality hand-crafted toys for youngsters, such as Nantucket mermaids, and children's books based on local themes, such as Joan Aiken's brilliant *Nightbirds on Nantucket.*

*From her quiet spot on the sand at Jetties Beach, a young woman looks up from her novel at the scene: Although it is fall, three colorful Windsurfers streak across the water, inured to the breeze in their wetsuits; a couple arrive on matching mountain bikes, each with binoculars strung around their necks; a family with a totebag filled with snacks investigates the shoreline possibly in search of shells, or farther out, seals. This is the default setting of the beach, when from October through May nary a beach umbrella nor sun bather is in sight.*

## In This Chapter



*Revised and updated by Linda Hammes and Bill Maple*

# outdoor activities and sports

**WHEN THE PHRASE "THE GREAT OUTDOORS" WAS COINED,** its author must have had Nantucket on her mind. The island setting is downright seductive, so let yourself be wooed, and come out and play. On Nantucket one can spot sophisticated urban children and their typically very composed parents get excited about spotting a bird fly up out of the grasslands, or detecting a whale's tail rising out of the sea or watching the cranberries float to the top of a bog. Gardening is practically the island sport, as are biking, sailing, and hiking. Here even an unremarkable game of frisbee or a ball toss on the beach becomes a memorable experience imparted by the stunning setting. Whether on land, shore, or sea, let Nantucket inspire your inner naturalist, adventure-seeker, or athlete—and take her outside.

## BEACHES

A calm area by the harbor, **Children's Beach** (S. Beach St.) is an easy walk east from town, and it's perfect for small children. The beach has a grassy park with benches, a playground, lifeguards, food service, picnic tables, showers, and rest rooms. Tie-dyeing lessons are offered Friday at noon mid-July–August.

**Cisco** (Hummock Pond Rd., South Shore) is a long, sandy beach with heavy surf, lifeguards, and rest rooms. It's not easy to get to from Nantucket Town, though. There are no bike trails to it, so you may need to walk or take a taxi. Also, the cliffs are severely

## Sand-Castle and Sculpture Days

*Buddhas; dragons; mermaids; and, of course, whales inhabit Jetties Beach during the annual Sandcastle Sculpture Contest in August. Creative concoctions, often with maritime themes, emerge from the sand: fish, porpoises, submarines, and crabs are common enough, although they're frequently constructed with a touch of whimsy, as in a giant, man-eating clam. Automobiles, spaceships, celestial bodies, flowers, and the famous lightship baskets are carefully and creatively crafted out of sand, shells, seaweed, and even beach litter. You might even see a castle or two! Anyone can stake out a patch of sand. There are prizes in several age groups and categories, so grab a shovel, bucket, turkey baster (a secret weapon for blowing sand), rake, and sunscreen and join the fun. Registration forms are available at the Chamber office, 24 Main Street.*

eroded, so getting down onto the beach is difficult. Still, the waves make it a popular spot for body- and boardsurfers.

**Dionis Beach** (Eel Point Rd.) is, at its entrance, a narrow strip of sand that turns into a wider, more private strand with high dunes and fewer children. The beach has a rocky bottom; calm, rolling waters; lifeguards; and rest rooms. Take the Madaket Bike Path to Eel Point Road Path and look for a white rock pointing to the beach, about 3 mi west of town.

Six miles from Nantucket Town and accessible only by foot, **Eel Point** (Eel Point Rd. off Cliff Rd., near Madaket) has one of the island's most beautiful and interesting beaches for those who don't necessarily need to swim—a sandbar extends out 100 yards, keeping the water shallow, clear, and calm. There are no services, just lots of birds, wild berries and bushes, and solitude.

**Jetties Beach** (Hulbert Ave. 1½ mi northwest of Straight Wharf), a short bike or shuttle-bus ride from town, is the most popular beach for families because of its calm surf, lifeguards, bathhouse, rest rooms, and snack bar. It's a lively scene, especially with passing ferries, water-sports rentals (Windsurfer, sailboat, kayak), a playground and volleyball nets on the beach, and tennis courts adjacent. Swim lessons for children age 6 and up are offered daily 9:30–noon, July 4–Labor Day. It's a good place to try out water toys—kayaks, sailboards, and day-sailers—since the water is gentle. The concessions and rest rooms are wheelchair-accessible, and there is a boardwalk to the beach.

Known for great sunsets and surf, **Madaket Beach** (Madaket) is reached by shuttle bus from Nantucket Town or the Madaket Bike Path (5½ mi) and has lifeguards and rest rooms.

**Siasconset Beach** (end of Milestone Rd.), also known as 'Sconset Beach and Codfish Park, has a golden-sand beach with moderate to heavy surf, a lifeguard, showers, rest rooms, and a playground. Restaurants are a short walk away.

**Surfside** (Surfside Rd., South Shore) is the island's premier surf beach, with lifeguards, rest rooms, a snack bar, and a wide strand of sand. It pulls in college students as well as families and is great for kite flying and surf casting. You can take the Surfside Bike Path or the shuttle here.

## BIKING

One of the best ways to tour Nantucket is by bicycle. Miles of paved bike paths wind through all types of terrain from one end of the island to the other; it is possible to bike around the entire island in a day. Most paths start within ½ mi of town, and all are well marked with different-color trail-route indicators. Several lead to beaches and have drinking fountains and benches placed in strategic spots along the way. And if you're without

your wheels, it's easy enough to rent some (☞ Bike Shops, *below*). The paths are also perfect for runners and bladers.

## Bike Paths

The new **Eel Point Road Path** starts at the junction of Eel Point Road and Madaket Road. It's over a mile long and makes Dionis Beach (☞ *above*) to the west more accessible.

The **Milestone Bike Path,** linking Nantucket Town and 'Sconset, is probably the least scenic of the paths but is still quite pleasant. When paired with the Polpis Path it becomes a 20-mi island loop.

The **Madaket Path** route starts at the intersection of Quaker and Madaket roads and takes you out to Madaket Beach, on the island's west end. This route encompasses the Madaket and Cliff Road bike paths and is about 12 mi round-trip, easily doable in an afternoon.

The 8-mi **Polpis Bike Path,** a long trail with gentle hills, begins at the intersection of Milestone and Polpis Roads and winds alongside Polpis Road almost all the way into 'Sconset. It goes right by the Nantucket Life Saving Museum (☞ Here and There) and has great views of the moors, the cranberry bogs, and Sesachacha Pond.

The 6½-mi **'Sconset Bike Path** starts at the rotary east of Nantucket Town and parallels Milestone Road, ending in 'Sconset. It is paved and mostly level, with some gentle hills and benches as well as drinking fountains at strategic locations along the way.

The easy 3½-mi **Surfside Bike Path,** which begins on Surfside Road (from Main Street take Pleasant Street; then turn right onto Atlantic Avenue), leads to Surfside, the island's premier ocean beach (☞ *above*). Benches and drinking fountains are spaced along the path.

## Keeping Wildlife Wild

*Nantucket and the nearby islands of Tuckernuck and Muskeget host a unique community of plants and animals. The largely treeless expanse of sand-plain grassland and coastal heath (also called moors) along Nantucket's southern half is the world's largest of its kind. In this setting of stark beauty are a number of species in the rhododendron or heath family: blueberry, huckleberry, and bearberry. In addition to the heath are forests, swamps, salt marshes, and barrier beaches.*

*When the 1960s tourism boom began, it was clear that something had to be done to preserve the miles of heath-covered moors and clean, white-sand beaches. Led by the Nantucket Conservation Foundation (NCF), established in 1963, organizations such as the Trustees of Reservations, the Land Bank, and the Massachusetts Audubon Society have acquired through purchase or gift more than 8,500 acres, including working cranberry bogs and great tracts of moorland for conservation. Now about 40% of this rare habitat is protected from development and all of it is open to the public for hikes, nature study, and scientific research. Much of it is crossed by dirt roads and many hiking trails.*

*Take your binoculars and camera and walk the trails of Sanford Farm or the moors around Altar Rock. If you're observant you'll certainly spy the Northern harrier gliding low over the hummocks in search of a meal, and, if you're lucky, you might catch a glimpse of the endangered short-eared owl. The absence of typical ground-dwelling predators such as weasels and coyote makes Nantucket a haven for ground-nesting birds such as these as well as several species of gulls and terns. Around your feet you might also see the American burying beetle, Northeastern beach tiger beetle, bushy rock rose, and wood lily. In spring and early summer some beaches are closed to vehicles and have restricted pedestrian access in order to protect the nests and chicks of least terns and piping plovers.*

# Glossary of Birds

## BIRDS

Nantucket's unique heath is home to a number of plants and animals that are less common elsewhere. Those that are rare, endangered, or of special concern are indicated by an asterisk (*). Scientific names are in italics.

**American oystercatcher.** *Haematopus palliatus.* This noisy shore bird has a black back, white belly, and bright red bill.

**Common yellowthroat.** *Geothlypis trichas.* This warbler has a dark back and yellow belly. The male has a distinct black mask and sings a song described as "witchity-witchity."

**Great Egret.** *Casmerodius albus.* This large, white heron has a light-colored bill and black legs and feet.

***Least tern.** *Sterna albifrons.* This is the smallest tern species. It has a white forehead and yellow feet and bill and flies with very rapid wing beats.

***Northern harrier.** *Circus cyaneus.* This hawk glides easily just above the moors. Watch for the distinctive white rump patch as it tilts in its flight. The males are gray; the females, brown.

***Piping plover.** *Charadrius melodus.* This small, pale shore bird has a complete or incomplete dark ring around the neck. The legs are yellow, and the beak is yellow with a dark tip.

**Red-tailed hawk.** *Buteo jamaicensis.* This large hawk with broad, rounded wings has a distinctive rust-color tail and soars higher than the harrier (☞ *above*).

**Savannah sparrow.** *Passerculus sandwichensis.* This sparrow makes its home in open heathland and has a short, notched tail; a yellow eye stripe; and a streaked breast.

**Snowy egret.** *Egretta thula.* Smaller than the great egret (☞ *above*), this species has a dark beak, black legs, and yellow feet.

# Glossary of Common Wildflowers

## WILDFLOWERS

**Bearberry.** *Arctostaphylos uva-ursi.* A common, ground-hugging, evergreen vine whose white, bell-shape spring flowers produce red berries during the summer.

***Bushy rockrose.** *Helianthemum dumosum.* A flower of the heath with five yellow petals and opposite leaves.

**Lady's slipper orchid.** *Cypripedium acaule.* A woodland species with a distinctive orchidlike pink flower.

***New England blazing star.** *Liatris scariosa.* A late-summer and fall aster with large, purple, fuzzy flowers ascending the stem.

**Racemed milkwort.** *Polygala polygama.* Small purple flowers distributed along a stalk; grows in clumps.

**Rugosa rose; wrinkled rose.** *Rosa rugosa.* White to deep magenta flowers. A typical rose with dense thorns on the stem and a thick "wrinkled" leaf. Common near sea shores and in dunes.

**Sea lavender.** *Limonium carolinianum.* This common salt-marsh plant looks like a tiny tree with abundant, small blue flowers.

**Wood lily.** *Lilium philadelphicum.* This distinct, upright, bright red-orange lily is found in the moors.

**Yellow ox-eye daisy; Marguerite.** *Chrysanthemum leucanthemum.* A tall, white-petaled daisy with a distinct yellow center.

## Bike Shops

**Nantucket Bike Shop** (Steamboat Wharf and Straight Wharf, tel. 508/228–1999 for both), open April–October, rents bicycles and mopeds and provides an excellent touring map. Daily rentals cost $12 for a children's bike and $18–$30 for an adult size, $45–$70 for a moped, though half- and multiple-day rates are available. Ask about free delivery and pickup.

**Young's Bicycle Shop** (Steamboat Wharf, 6 Broad St., tel. 508/228–1151), established in 1931, rents several different types of bicycle ($25–$35 daily), plus cars ($74–$125 daily) and Jeep Wranglers ($179 daily); multiple-day rates are available. The knowledgeable third-generation Young family and staff will send you off with everything you need—an excellent touring map, a helmet, and a picturesque little Portuguese basket for your handlebars.

# BIRD-WATCHING

More than 354 species flock to the island's moors, meadows, and marshes in the course of a year. Birds that are rare in other parts of New England thrive here due to the lack of predators and the abundance of wide-open, undeveloped space. Northern harriers, short-eared owls, and Savannah sparrows nest in the grasslands; oystercatchers, gulls, plovers, and tiny least terns nest on sands and in beach grasses; snowy egrets, great blue herons, and ospreys stalk the marshlands; and ring-necked pheasants, mockingbirds, and Carolina wrens inhabit the tangled bogs and thickets. Almost anywhere outside of town you're sure to see interesting bird life (☞ Bird-Watching Spots, *below*), not just in migratory season but year-round.

**Birding Adventures** (tel. 508/228–2703) has tours led by a naturalist who can wax eloquent on everything from raptors to oystercatchers.

## Bird-Watching Spots

*Set up your spotting scope near the salt marsh at Eel Point any time of year and you're bound to see shore birds feeding. They're particularly abundant during fall migration starting in July. Cross the dunes to the ocean side in spring to see nesting piping plovers and least terns. Folger's Marsh near the Life Saving Museum and the Harbor Flats at the end of Washington Street are also good shore-bird-watching sites. Inland, a walk through Sanford Farm from Madaket Road to the south shore traversing upland, forest, heath, and shore habitats, will bring you in range of Savannah sparrows, yellow warblers, osprey, and red-tailed hawks. Be on the lookout for the protected Northern harrier and the endangered short-eared owl. For woodland species, check out the trails through Windswept Cranberry Bog or the Masquetuck Reservation near Polpis Harbor.*

The **Maria Mitchell Association** (MMA; 2 Vestal St., tel. 508/228–9198) leads marine ecology field trips and wildflower and bird walks from June to Labor Day.

# OUTDOOR ACTIVITIES AND SPORTS

## Boating

### BOAT CHARTERS

The **Christina** (Slip 19, Straight Wharf, tel. 508/325–4000) is a classic brass and mohogany sailboat, for adventure excursions with the children or a private picnic-and-champagne sail to a cove along Coatue. Daily trips cost $25 and depart at 10 and 11:30 AM and 1, 2:30, 4, and 5:30 PM. A sunset trip also leaves daily at 7 and costs $35.

## Yachting Culture

*During July and August, Nantucket is the place to study, close-up, the world's possibly most splendid yachts—and the well-to-do people who own and sail them. Quaint, vintage motor yachts and sloops are moored fo'c's'le (forecastle) to stern with multitier, fiberglass cruisers and sleek racing yawls. Don't be surprised if you see yachts with piggyback motor launches, automobiles, and helicopters. Some of the most expensive slips on the East Coast attract vessels bearing flags and registries from around the world. Most of them spend a few days here, many from a tour that originated in the Mediterranean via the Caribbean. Even if you're not usually interested in boats, come visit the Straight, Old South, and Commercial wharves to observe the conditions under which these poor yachters are forced to live.*

The **Endeavor** (Slip 15, Straight Wharf, tel. 508/228–5585, May–Oct.), a charter replica Friendship sloop, makes four daily 1½-hour trips out to the jetties and into the sound. Departures are at 10, 1, and 4 ($22.50 per person), and a sunset cruise ($30 per person) leaves at 5:30.

### BOAT RENTALS

**Nantucket Boat Rental** (Slip 1, Straight Wharf, tel. 508/325–1001) rents powerboats ($1,500 deposit). Security deposits are required for all boat rentals, and boats 17 ft or more require previous boating experience. Smaller crafts (13 and 17 ft) are limited to the harbor and five passengers; 20- and 22-ft crafts may hold up to 10.

**Nantucket Harbor Sail** (Swain's Wharf, tel. 508/228–0424) rents 19-ft sailboats ($80 2 hrs, $130 4 hrs, $200 per day). Security deposits are not required, although previous boating experience is.

**Nantucket Island Community Sailing** (Jetties Beach, tel. 508/ 228–5358, 508/228–6600, or 508/228–9226) rents Sunfish, Windsurfers, and kayaks; it also runs two-week sailing sessions at Polpis Harbor and adult sailing classes.

**Sea Nantucket** (Washington St. ¼ mi southeast of Commercial Wharf, tel. 508//228–7499) rents kayaks ($15–$30) and small sailboats ($30–$50) by the half or full hour at the vest-pocket Francis Street Beach.

## Dance Lessons

**Dance Nantucket** (tel. 508/325–6679, www.dancenantucket.org; call for location) hosts dance performances and leads classes in Latin, swing, and ballroom for all levels.

**Giovanna La Paglia** (10 Surfside Rd., tel. 508/228–4979) directs a ballet studio for children and adults at the Cyrus Pierce Middle School; recitals often feature professional guest dancers.

**Leslie Farlow** (tel. 508/257–6629), director of the dance program at Trinity College, offers summertime instruction in modern dance, yoga, and drama. Call for location.

**Marjorie Trott** (8 Dukes Rd., tel. 508/228–4209) teaches popular classes in creative movement and drama for children ages 1–9 at various venues, including the Children's Beach bandstand (off Harbor View Way) in-season and the Atheneum (1 India St.) off-season.

## Fishing

Surf fishing is very popular on Nantucket, especially in the late spring when bluefish are running. Blues and bass are the main island catches—bluefishing is best at Great Point—but there

are plentiful numbers of other flavorful fish as well. Fresh-water fishing is also an option at many area ponds.

**Barry Thurston's Fishing Tackle** (Harbor Sq., tel. 508/228–9595) has lots of fishing tips and rents all the gear you'll need. Mike Monte also arranges independent surf- and fly-fishing tours via a four-wheel-drive vehicle to the outer beaches.

**Bill Fisher Tackle** (14 New La., tel. 508/228–2261) sells and rents equipment and can point you in the direction of the best fishing spots.

**Herbert T.** (Slip 14, Straight Wharf, tel. 508/228–6655) and other boats are available for seasonal charter from Straight Wharf for sport-fishing tours and excursions.

**Whitney Mitchell** (tel. 508/228–2331) leads guided surf-casting trips with tackle by four-wheel-drive.

### FISHING LICENSES

Fishing licenses are needed only for fresh-water fishing and shellfishing. **Fresh-water licenses** can be obtained at local fishing outfitters or through the Marine, Harbormaster, and Shellfish Department (34 Washington St., tel. 508/228–7260).

The **shellfish warden** (34 Washington St., tel. 508/228–7260) issues digging permits for littleneck and cherrystone clams, quahogs, and mussels. Family shellfishing permits are $15.

## Golf

**Miacomet Golf Club** (12 W. Miacomet Ave., off Somerset La., tel. 508/325–0333), a public course owned by the Land Bank and abutting Miacomet and Hummock ponds and coastal heathland, has nine holes on very flat terrain.

**Sankaty Head Golf Club** (Polpis Rd., 'Sconset, tel. 508/257–6391), a private 18-hole course, is open to the public Columbus Day through Memorial Day. This challenging Scottish-style links course cuts through the moors and has spectacular views of the lighthouse and ocean from practically every hole.

**Siasconset Golf Club** (Milestone Rd., tel. 508/257–6596), begun in 1894, is an easy-walking nine-hole public course surrounded by conservation land.

## Fitness Clubs

**Nantucket Health Club** (10 Young's Way, tel. 508/228–4750) has StairMasters, Lifecycles, treadmills, rowers, Airdyne bikes, New Generation Nautilus, and free weights; aerobics and yoga classes; and personal trainers. You can get a short-term pass that covers the machines, fitness classes, or both.

**Brant Point Runners Club** (tel. 508/228–4830) isn't actually a place; it's a group of folks who get together every Tuesday at 5:30 May–October for a 3.1-mi run. Just show up at the corner of Beach and Easton streets.

## Hiking and Conservation Areas

The island of Nantucket has a fascinating array of landscapes—wild, open tracts of bog land and moors; groves of scrub oak and pitch pine; and wide, sandy beaches that stretch seemingly forever. A diverse assortment of plant and animal species, many of which are endangered or threatened, thrive here as nowhere else. The windswept heathlands that compose much of Nantucket's acreage are becoming globally rare and are protected on the island by various conservation organizations that use carefully controlled fires to burn away encroaching shrubs and trees. Flowering plants are especially prolific after these burns and include such rare species as bush rockrose, pink lady's slipper, and the Eastern silvery aster.

Other local species of flora and fauna to keep watch for are the white flowers of the Nantucket shadbush, brilliant red cardinal flowers, bird's-foot violets, false heather, pink Virginia roses, wild morning glories, and big, beautiful red-orange wood lilies; in the fall, look for asters, goldenrod, and the tall purple spikes and thistlelike flowers of the endangered New England blazing star. Although cranberries are the most abundant berry, there are also blueberries, raspberries, blackberries, and huckleberries. Beach plums, beach peas, and the fragrant non-native rosa rugosa grow well near the sea in the sandiest soil. In the meadows and groves are mice, moles, meadow voles, white-tailed deer, and cottontail rabbits—and a distinct lack of predatory mammals such as raccoons, skunks, and opossums due to Nantucket's distance from the mainland. On the beach and in the sea, mollusks such as oysters, mussels, steamers, quahogs, and blue crabs are plentiful and can be harvested as long as you have the proper shellfishing permit (☞ Fishing Licenses, *above*).

Please remember that these conservation areas are set aside to preserve and protect Nantucket's fragile ecosystems—tread carefully.

## Miniature Golf

**Nobadeer Minigolf** (Nobadeer Farm and Sun Island Rds. off Milestone Rd., tel. 508/228–8977), an 18-hole miniature golf course is reached by a path connecting with the 'Sconset Bike Path. Admission is $6, and it's open daily 9 AM–11 PM June–September. There's also a shuttle from downtown ($1).

## Scuba Diving

The scuba diving around Nantucket is somewhat limited. Visibility is often only 5 ft, and there are no spectacular wrecks to visit. Most diving is done off the jetties. The **Sunken Ship** (Broad and S. Water Sts., tel. 508/228–9226) has complete dive-shop services, including lessons, guided dives, equipment rentals, and charters; it also rents water skis, boogie boards, and fishing poles.

## Swimming

The Olympic-size, indoor **Nantucket Community Pool** (Nantucket High School, 10 Surfside Rd., tel. 508/228–7262) is open daily year-round for lap and recreational swimming and lessons.

The **Summer House** (☞ Where to Stay) in 'Sconset offers its pool, on the bluff above the ocean beach, to diners at its poolside café in season.

## Tennis

There are six asphalt **town courts** (tel. 508/325–5334) at Jetties Beach. Sign up at the Park and Recreation Commission building for one hour of court time (usually the limit) or for lessons or tennis clinics. There is a charge for court maintenance: $15 per hour for singles, $20 per hour for doubles.

**Brant Point Racquet Club** (48 N. Beach St., tel. 508/228–3700), a short walk from town, has nine fast-dry clay courts and a pro shop and offers lessons, rentals, playing programs, and round-robins.

**Siasconset Casino** (10 New St., 'Sconset, tel. 508/257–6661) is a private club with seven clay courts and four soft-green Har-tru courts. Non-members openings are at 1–2 and 2–3, but you should call ahead. Private lessons can be arranged at any time.

## Yoga

**Nantucket Health Club** (☞ *above*) has yoga classes.

**Shannah Green** (tel. 508/228–9627; call for directions) teaches nine classes a week during summer and six a week the rest of year, plus the occasional workshop. Group classes are 1¼ hours and cost $10 each. All levels are welcome; private lessons can be arranged.

**Sheri Perelman** (tel. 508/325–0763; call for directions), Kripalu certified, leads yoga classes or private sessions year-round from a small mid-island studio. Classes are generally held Monday, Wednesday, and Friday at 8:30 AM and 5:30 PM, and cost $15 per class; in summer you can buy eight classes for $100.

# GUIDED TOURS

## CRUISES

Boats of all kinds leave from Straight Wharf on harbor sails throughout the summer; many are available for charter as well.

**Anna W. II** (Slip 12, tel. 508/228–1444) is a renovated lobster boat with shoreline, sunset, and moonlight cruises, as well as lobstering demonstrations and winter seal cruises.

The **"Around the Sound"** cruise, a one-day round-trip from Hyannis with stops at Nantucket and Martha's Vineyard and six hours at sea, is available June–mid-September. *Hy-Line, Ocean St. Dock, Hyannis, tel. 508/778–2600; 508/778–2602; or 508/228–3949 on Nantucket. $33, bicycles $15.*

The **Endeavor** (Slip 15, tel. 508/228–5585), a beautiful 31-ft Friendship sloop, offers harbor tours, sunset cruises, and sails to Coatue, where you are rowed ashore to spend a morning beachcombing.

**Nantucket Whale Watch** (Hy-Line dock, Straight Wharf, tel. 508/283–0313 or 800/322–0013) naturalists lead full-day excursions on the *Yankee Sleet* Tuesday and Friday mid-July–August. The cost is $88 for adults, $48 for children, and reservations are essential.

The 40-ft sailing yacht **Sparrow** (Slip 18, tel. 508/228–6029), with a teak, brass, and stained-glass interior, offers 1½-hour sails for six guests, plus charters.

## GENERAL TOURS

**Barrett's Tours** (20 Federal St., tel. 508/228–0174 or 800/773–0174) gives 75- to 90-minute narrated bus tours of the island from spring through fall; the Barrett family has lived on Nantucket for generations. Buses meet the ferries; reservations aren't necessary.

**Carried Away** (tel. 508/228–0218) offers narrated carriage rides through the town historic district in season.

**Gail's Tours** (tel. 508/257–6557) are lively 1½-hour van tours narrated by sixth-generation Nantucketer Gail Johnson, who knows all the inside stories.

**"Historic Nantucket Walking Tours,"** a free, self-guided tour pamphlet published by the Nantucket Historical Association (NHA), is available at the Nantucket Information Bureau (☞ Practical Information). In season, tours are led daily at 10:30 and 2:30 by an NHA docent and meet at the Whaling Museum. Call for reservations or off-season times.

**Nantucket Island Tours** (Straight Wharf, tel. 508/228–0334) gives 75- to 90-minute narrated bus tours of the island from spring through fall; buses meet the ferries.

## HISTORICAL TOURS

The self-guided **Black Heritage Trail** tour (Box 1802, Nantucket 02544, tel. 508/228–4058) covers nine sites in and around Nantucket Town that have associations with Nantucket's African-American population, including the African Meeting House, the Whaling Museum, and the Atheneum. The trail guide is free from the Friends of the African Meeting House on Nantucket.

## NATURE TOURS

**Great Point Natural History Tours** (tel. 508/228–6799), led by naturalists, are sponsored by the Trustees of Reservations. Groups drive in for the three-hour tour, with stops to see points of interest and certain bird species, and to stretch.

For a map of the **Nantucket Conservation Foundation**'s properties, visit or write NCF headquarters. The map costs $3, or $4 by mail. *118 Cliff Rd., Box 13, Nantucket 02554, tel. 508/228–2884. Weekdays 8–5.*

*The trip over on the ferry provides a calming view of deep blue water and the salty scent of a gentle breeze—but passengers are anything but languorous as they approach Nantucket. Most are chatting away about how they'll spend the day: a young couple is carrying the picnic basket they'll unpack at a lighthouse; a well-dressed woman of a certain age talks with her friends about visiting the shops on Petticoat Row; a girl of about 12 asks her father if they can stop by the observatory later that night. But one visitor is silent; she and her bike, her only companion on this clear sunny day, plan a slow ride out to the dunes with nothing more strenuous in mind than watching the tide come in.*

## In This Chapter



*Revised and updated by Elizabeth Gehrman*

# here and there

**IN ADDITION TO NANTUCKET'S CRANBERRY BOGS** and fields of daffodils, there are dozens of lovely and interesting man-made sights to see, from a working windmill to a passel of lighthouses; from the Quaker Friends Meeting House to the centuries-old Greek Revival town houses. In fact, in 1972, the entire island was declared a historic district—800 buildings predate the Civil War—and it's one of the country's finest.

On a magnificent harbor, Nantucket Town remains the center of island activity as it has since the early 1700s. A small commercial area of a few square blocks leads up from the waterfront. Beyond it, quiet residential roads fan out to points around the island; Siasconset ('Sconset) lies 7 mi to the east, Surfside 3 mi to the south, and Madaket 6 mi west of town. During your stay, also look for guided house-and-garden tours, as well as lectures in astronomy, nautical lore, and more.

*Numbers in the text correspond to numbers in the margin and on the Nantucket Town Sightseeing map.*

## NANTUCKET TOWN

With so many landmarks packed into a small area, Nantucket Town is perfect for an afternoon stroll or a serious walking tour. Either way, you'll pass a couple dozen historical sights while taking in the lovely gardens, imposing Greek Revival buildings, cobblestone streets, and salty sea air. If you're staying all summer, you might want to buy a pass from the Nantucket Historical Association (☞ *below*) and the Maria Mitchell

# nantucket town sightseeing

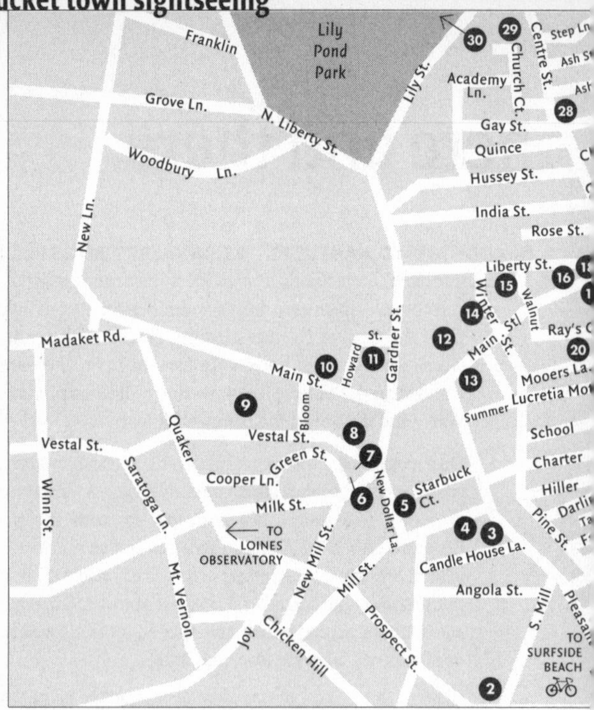


African Meeting House, **1**
Atheneum, **23**
Coffin houses, **16**
Coffin School, **14**
Dreamland Theatre, **24**
1800 House, **4**
Fire Hose Cart House, **11**
First Congregational Church, **29**
Greater Light, **10**
Hadwen House, **13**
Hinchman House, **6**
Jared Coffin House, **28**
John Wendell Barrett House, **17**
Macy-Christian House, **15**
Maria Mitchell Science Library, **7**
Mitchell House, **8**
Moors' End, **3**
Nantucket Information Bureau, **27**
Old Gaol, **9**
Old Mill, **2**
Oldest House, **30**
Pacific Club, **19**
Pacific National Bank, **18**

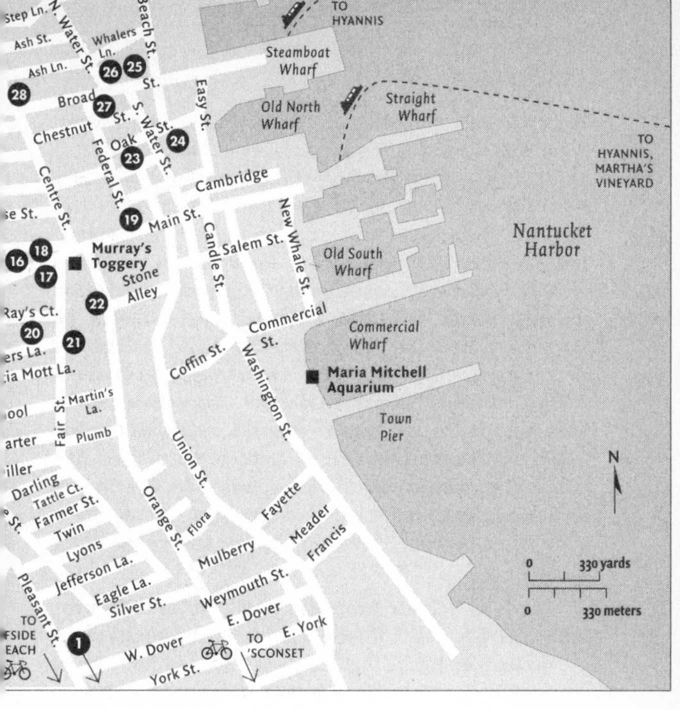


Peter Foulger Museum, **26**

Quaker Meeting House, **20**

St. Paul's Episcopal Church, **21**

Starbuck refinery and candle works, **5**

"Three Bricks," **12**

Unitarian Universalist Church, **22**

Whaling Museum, **25**

Association (☞ *below*) for discounted admission to several sights.

## A Good Walk

Begin your walk at the **African Meeting House** ①, which dates to the 1880s, when it was a cultural center for emancipated slaves. Head east on Prospect Street, past the island's only remaining windmill, **Old Mill** ②, and turn left on South Mill. At Pleasant Street, take a left. At Candle House Lane is **Moors' End** ③, a 1834 Federal-style house. Turning left at Mill Street, you'll find quite a different kind of structure, the simple **1800 House** ④. Follow New Dollar Lane, past the remains of the **Starbuck refinery and candle works** ⑤, toward Vestal Street and the Maria Mitchell Association's **Hinchman House Natural Science Museum** ⑥, **Maria Mitchell Association Street Science Library** ⑦, and **Mitchell House** ⑧, as well as the 1805 **Old Gaol** ⑨. Backtrack a bit, take a right onto Bloom Street, and take another right on Main for Howard Street; No. 8 is **Greater Light** ⑩ and a good example of an early artist's house. Then, round the corner onto Gardner Street to see the **Fire Hose Cart House** ⑪.

Walking from Gardner Street along Main Street toward the harbor, you'll find the **"Three Bricks"** ⑫ on Upper Main Street and the **Hadwen House** ⑬ at No. 96. In 1846 a fire destroyed all of the simple Quaker buildings in the downtown area, and many were rebuilt in brick, in the Federal and Greek Revival styles that were prevalent on the mainland at the time. Peek down Winter Street for a look at the **Coffin School** ⑭ and down Liberty Street for the **Macy-Christian House** ⑮ as you head toward the **Coffin houses** ⑯ at 75 and 78 Main Street, the **John Wendell Barrett House** ⑰ at No. 72, the **Pacific National Bank** ⑱ at 62 Main Street, and the **Pacific Club** ⑲ at Main and Federal streets. Petticoat Row (☞ Petticoat Row *below*), a historical shopping district, runs along Centre Street north of Main Street. South of Main Street are several houses of worship: the **Quaker Meeting**

**House** ⑳, **St. Paul's Episcopal Church** ㉑, and the **Unitarian Universalist Church** ㉒. A bit of whimsy is found on the wall of the last building on the left on Washington Street, at Main Street: a sign listing distances from Nantucket to various points of the globe. It's 14,650 mi to Tahiti, in case you were wondering.

From Main Street head north on Federal Street for the **Atheneum** ㉓, Nantucket's 1847 library, at 1 Lower India Street, and the **Dreamland Theatre** ㉔. If you're just getting your bearings, now's probably a good time to pick up a bike map from the **Nantucket Information Bureau** ㉗ as you head east for a block at the Easy Street Boat Basin. Grab a bench and watch the ferries come and go. After your respite, head for the superb **Whaling Museum** ㉕ and neighboring **Peter Foulger Museum** ㉖ on Broad Street—try to time your arrival to catch the lectures offered at both. Then head west on Broad Street to the **Jared Coffin House** ㉘. Take a right onto Centre Street for the island's most elegant church, **First Congregational Church** ㉙. Just beyond it is **Oldest House** ㉚, a point of interest for architecture buffs.

### TIMING

Depending on how how long you choose to linger in the museums and shops you'll pass, this walk might take anywhere from two hours to a day.

## What to See

As far back as the early 1700s, there was a small African-American population on Nantucket; the earliest blacks were slaves of the island's first settlers. When slavery was abolished on the island in 1773, Nantucket became a destination for free blacks and escaping slaves. Today nine sights associated with the island's African-American heritage are on the self-guided Black Heritage Trail tour
❶ (☞ Tours in Practical Information). Of these, the **African Meeting House** is the only extant public building constructed and occupied by African-Americans in the 19th century. Built in the 1820s as a

schoolhouse, it functioned as such until 1848 when the island's schools were integrated. Then, and until 1911, the building was used as a church. A complete restoration, both inside and out, has returned the site to its authentic 1880s appearance. Rooms for lectures, concerts, and readings help to preserve the contributions and experiences of African-Americans on Nantucket. *York and Pleasant Sts., tel. 508/228–9833 or 617/725–0022. Suggested donation $2. July–Aug., Tues.–Sat. 11–3, Sun. 1–3.*

The great white Greek Revival building with the odd windowless
23 facade and fluted Ionic columns is the **Atheneum,** Nantucket's town library. Completed in 1847 to replace a structure lost to the fire, this is one of the oldest libraries in continuous service in the United States. The astronomer Maria Mitchell (☞ Mitchell House, *below*) was its first librarian. Opening ceremonies included a dedication by Ralph Waldo Emerson, who—along with Daniel Webster, Henry David Thoreau, Frederick Douglass, Lucretia Mott, and John James Audubon—later delivered lectures in the library's second-floor Great Hall. During the 19th century the hall was the center of island culture, hosting public meetings, suffrage rallies, and county fairs. Because of its history, and its beautiful restoration, the Atheneum is a pleasure to visit. Check out the periodicals section on the second floor to get all the local news. A morning story hour is held weekly; call ahead for the schedule. The adjoining Atheneum Park is a wonderful spot in which to read. *1 Lower India St., tel. 508/228–1110. Memorial Day–Labor Day, Mon., Wed., and Fri.–Sat. 9:30–5, Tues. and Thurs. 9:30–8; Labor Day–Memorial Day, Tues. and Thurs. 9:30–8, Wed. and Fri.–Sat. 9:30–5.*

---

OFF THE BEATEN PATH

The 26-ft-tall, white-painted **Brant Point Light** has views of the harbor and town and a tiny beach from which to watch boats coming and going. The point was the site of the second-oldest lighthouse in the country (1746), though the present, much-photographed light was built in 1902. In fact, the existing lighthouse is the 10th to occupy this historic spot; its reassuring beacon is visible from 10 mi offshore. *End of Easton St., across a footbridge.*

You might want to stop at the **Chamber of Commerce** to get your bearings. You'll find maps and island information available year-round. *Upstairs at 48 Main St., tel. 508/228–1700. Weekdays 9–5.*

16 The two attractive brick **Coffin houses,** the Henry Coffin House and the Charles G. Coffin House, face each other and were built for brothers. The Coffins were wealthy shipping agents and whale-oil merchants who used the same mason for these 1830s houses and the later Three Bricks (☞ *above*). The houses are privately owned and not open to the public. *75 and 78 Main St.*

14 The impressive Greek Revival **Coffin School** was built in 1884 to house a school founded nearly six decades earlier by Admiral Sir Isaac Coffin to train the youth of Nantucket (at the time, virtually all were Coffin descendants) in the ways of the sea. (Although by this time, the whaling industry had fizzled out.) Since 1996 it has been home to the Egan Institute of Maritime Studies, whose mission is to "advance the study and appreciation of the history, literature, art, and maritime traditions of Nantucket" through changing art exhibits, publications, and nautical instruction. *4 Winter St., tel. 508/228–2505. $1. Memorial Day–Columbus Day, daily 1–5.*

24 Currently a summer cinema, the handsome wooden **Dreamland Theatre** was built as a Quaker meetinghouse in 1829 and then became a straw factory and, later, an entertainment hall. It was moved to Brant Point as part of the grand Nantucket Hotel in the late 19th century and was floated across the harbor by barge in about 1905 to its present location—a good illustration of early Nantucketers' penchant for the multiple use of dwellings, as well as the relocation of houses. Trees (and therefore lumber) were so scarce that Herman Melville joked in *Moby-Dick* that "pieces of wood in Nantucket are carried about like bits of the true cross in Rome." *17 S. Water St., tel. 508/228–5356.*

4 The **1800 House** is a typical Nantucket home—one not enriched by whaling money—that shows how the other half lived at the time of its construction. Once the residence of the high sheriff, the house has locally made furniture and other household goods, a six-flue chimney with beehive oven, and a summer kitchen. Unfortunately, the NHA is restoring the house, so it will be closed in 2001. *10 Mill St., tel. 508/228–1894.*

Built in 1886 as one of several neighborhood fire stations—Nantucketers had learned their lesson after the 1846
11 conflagration—the **Fire Hose Cart House** displays a small collection of fire-fighting equipment used in the 18th century, including dousing buckets and a hand-pumped fire cart. *8 Gardner St., tel. 508/228–1894. Free. Memorial Day–Columbus Day, daily 10–5.*

★ 29 **First Congregational Church,** also known as the Old North Church, is Nantucket's largest and most elegant. Its tower—whose steeple is capped with a weather vane depicting a whale catch—rises 120 ft, providing the best view of Nantucket to be had. On a clear day the reward for climbing the 92 steps (many landings break the climb) is a panorama encompassing Great Point, Sankaty Head Lighthouse, Muskeget and Tuckernuck islands, moors, ponds, beaches, and the winding streets and rooftops of town. A peek at the church's interior reveals its old box pews, a turn-of-the-20th-century organ, and a trompe-l'oeil ceiling done by an unknown Italian painter in 1850 and since restored. (Organ aficionados may want to have a look at the 1831 Appleton—one of only four extant—at the United Methodist Church next to the Pacific National Bank on Main Street.) The Old North Vestry in the rear, the oldest house of worship on the island, was built in 1725 about a mile north of its present site. The main church was built in 1834. *62 Centre St., tel. 508/228–0950. Tour $2.50. Mid-June–mid-Oct., Mon.–Sat. 10–4; call for tower tours. Services Sun. at 8, 9, and 10:15 AM.*

10 A whimsical blend of necessity and creativity, **Greater Light** is an example of the summer homes of the artists who flocked to

Nantucket in its early resort days. In the 1930s two unusual Quaker sisters from Philadelphia—actress Hanna and artist Gertrude Monaghan—converted a barn into what now looks like the lavish set for an old movie. The exotic decor includes Italian furniture, Native American artifacts and textiles, a wrought-iron balcony, bas-reliefs, and a coat of arms. Unfortunately, it's closed to the public for renovations, although the adjacent garden is open. The sisters also remodeled the private house next door, called Lesser Light, for their parents. *8 Howard St.*

When you are touring Main Street, the magnificent white, porticoed Greek Revival mansions you'll see—referred to as the Two Greeks—were built in 1845 and 1846 by wealthy factory owner William Hadwen, a Newport native who made his money in whale oil and candles. No. 94, built as a wedding gift for his adopted niece, was modeled on the Athenian Tower of the Winds, with Corinthian capitals on the entry columns, a domed-stair hall with statuary niches, and an oculus. The Hadwens' own domicile, at No. 96, is
13 now a museum, the **Hadwen House,** which reflects how the wealthy of the period lived. The house has been restored to its mid-19th-century origins, with classic Victorian gas chandeliers and furnishings, as well as reproduction wallpapers and window treatments. Inside, on a tour, you'll see such architectural details as the grand circular staircase, fine plasterwork, and carved Italian-marble mantels. A second-floor gallery has exhibits that change annually; the 2000 show was about lightship baskets. Behind the house are period gardens. *96 Main St., tel. 508/228–1894. $3 or NHA pass. Memorial Day–Labor Day, daily 10–5; Labor Day–Columbus Day, daily 11–3.*

If you're interested in the natural history of Nantucket, the
6 **Hinchman House Natural Science Museum** displays specimens of local birds, insects, and plants and their local habitats. The museum also leads birding and wildflower walks and offers children's nature classes. The building houses the Maria Mitchell Association's gift shop as well. *7 Milk St., tel. 508/228–0898. $3 or MMA pass. Mid-June–mid-Sept., Tues.–Sat. 10–4.*

28 The handsome **Jared Coffin House** (☞ Eating Out *and* ☞ Where to Stay) has operated as an inn since the mid-19th century. Coffin was a wealthy merchant, and he built this brick house with Ionic portico, parapet, hip roof, and cupola—the only three-story structure on the island at the time—for his wife, who wanted to live closer to town. They moved here in 1845 from their home on Pleasant Street, but (so the story goes) nothing would please Mrs. Coffin, and within two years they left the island altogether for Boston. *29 Broad St., tel. 508/228–2400 or 800/248–2405.*

17 One of Nantucket's grand Main Street homes, the **John Wendell Barrett House** was built in 1820 in early Greek Revival style. Legend has it that Lydia Mitchell Barrett stood on the steps and refused to budge when, during the Great Fire, men tried to evacuate her so they could blow up the house to stop the spread of the fire. Luckily, a shift in the wind settled the showdown. *72 Main St.*

**Lily Pond Park,** a 5-acre conservation area on the edge of town, is a prime bird-watching spot. Its lawn and wetlands—there is a trail, but it's muddy—foster abundant wildlife, including birds, ducks, and deer. You can pick blackberries, raspberries, and grapes in season wherever you find them. *N. Liberty St.*

**Loines Observatory** (☞ Nightlife) hosts "open nights" on Wednesday night year-round, and more frequently in high season, so that you can get in a little stargazing. *Milk St. Ext., tel. 508/228–9198 or 508/228–9273. $10, or MMA pass. Mid-June–mid-Sept., Mon., Wed., and Fri. 9 PM–10:30 PM; Mid-Sept.–mid-June, Wed. and Fri. 8 PM–10:30 PM.*

---

NEED A BREAK? You can breakfast or lunch inexpensively at several soup-and-sandwich places, including **David's Soda Fountain** (Congdon's Pharmacy, 47 Main St., tel. 508/228–4549), where the local favorite is tuna salad.

**Nantucket Pharmacy** (45 Main St., tel. 508/228–0180) has a lunch counter that offers a quick, cheap, and simple lunch of mostly sandwiches. Try the excellent lobster roll.

Besides fresh-squeezed juices, the **Juice Bar** (12 Broad St., tel. 508/228–5799), open April to mid-October, serves homemade ice cream with waffle cones and lots of toppings. There are also baked goods, frozen yogurt, and specialty coffees. Long lines signal that good things come to those who wait.

---

15 The **Macy-Christian House,** a two-story lean-to built in 1745 for merchant Nathaniel Macy, has a great open hearth flanked by brick beehive ovens and old paneling. Part of the house reflects the late-19th-century Colonial Revival style of the 1934 renovation by the Christian family. The formal parlor and upstairs bedroom are in authentic Colonial style. *12 Liberty St., tel. 508/228–1894. $2 or NHA pass. Memorial Day–Labor Day, daily 10–5; Labor Day–Columbus Day, daily 11–3.*

The most-photographed view of **Main Street** is from the Pacific Club (☞ *below*). The cobblestone square has a harmonious symmetry: the Pacific Club anchors the foot of it, and the Pacific National Bank (☞ *below*), another redbrick building, squares off the head. The only broad thoroughfare in town, Main Street was widened after the Great Fire of 1846 leveled all its buildings except those made of brick, to safeguard against flames hopping across the street in the event of another fire. The cobblestones were brought to the island as ballast in returning ships and laid to prevent the wheels of carts heavily laden with whale oil from sinking into the dirt on their passage from the waterfront to the factories.

At the center of Lower Main is an old horse trough, today overflowing with flowers. From here the street gently rises. At the bank it narrows to its pre-fire width and leaves the commercial district for an area of mansions that escaped the blaze. The simple shop buildings that replaced those lost are a

pleasing hodgepodge of sizes, colors, and styles. Elm trees—thousands of which were planted in the 1850s by Henry and Charles Coffin—once formed a canopy over Main Street, but Dutch elm disease took most of them. In 1991 Hurricane Bob took two dozen more.

**Maria Mitchell Aquarium** fills its fresh- and saltwater tanks with local marine life, including flukes, skates, and lobsters. Children can pick up live crabs and starfish from the hands-on tank; family marine-ecology trips are given four times weekly in season. Renovations will soon triple the size of this popular maritime museum. *28 Washington St., near Commercial Wharf, tel. 508/228–5387. $1 or MMA pass. Mid-June–mid-Sept., Tues.–Sat. 10–4.*

The **Maria Mitchell Association (MMA),** established in 1902 by Vassar students and astronomer Maria Mitchell's family, administers the Mitchell House, the Maria Mitchell Science Library, the Hinchman House, the Maria Mitchell Aquarium, the Vestal Street Observatory, and the Loines Observatory. A combination admission ticket to the Mitchell House, the Hinchman House, the Vestal Street Observatory, and the aquarium is $7 for adults, and $5 for senior citizens and children ages 6–14. In summer, the association also offers inexpensive classes ($5) for adults and children on astronomy, natural science, and Nantucket history. *4 Vestal St., tel. 508/228–9198.*

7 The **Maria Mitchell Association (MMA) Science Library** has an extensive collection of science books and periodicals, including field guides and gardening books, as well as books on Nantucket history. *2 Vestal St., tel. 508/228–9219. Mid-June–mid-Sept., Tues.–Sat. 10–4; mid-Sept.–mid-June, Wed.–Fri. 2–5, Sat. 9–noon.*

8 Astronomy buffs will appreciate the **Mitchell House,** birthplace of astronomer and Vassar professor Maria (pronounced mah-*rye*-ah) Mitchell, who in 1847, at age 29, discovered a comet while surveying the sky from the top of the Pacific National Bank (☞ *below*). Her Quaker family had moved to quarters over the bank,

## Nantucket's Architectural Motifs

*Although "Nantucket" derives from a Native American word meaning "a land far out to sea," some of its most enduring symbols are solidly bound to terra firma, such as its architecture. The 2½-story typical Nantucket house, for example, is immediately identifiable by its gabled roof; traditional proportions; balanced window placement; and white cedar shingles, which in no time weather to their familiar mottled lead gray. The style took off in the 1760s and continued through the 1830s when Nantucket was largely a Quaker community. The house reflects the religion's minimalist aesthetic with simple design and careful craftsmanship.*

*Because the rooms were planned around a massive central chimney, the threat of fire was ever present and precautions were taken to guard against it. One such safeguard was to place transom lights over both the plank-frame front door and the interior doors; this created perpetual visual access to the interior. Similarly, roof walks, mistakenly known as widow's walks, were actually designed to allow access for putting out chimney fires. It was only later that the romantic notion developed of sea captains' wives pacing them as they watched the harbor for returning ships.*

*The ubiquitous shingles also had a practical purpose, as their tight covering (though only about 5 inches of shingle is visible, each board is 15 inches long) was the best protection against windy, rainy New England weather. Despite the additions that have been tacked on over the years, which Nantucketers grimly call "warts," many homes also still have the friendship stairs that lead both left and right from the front door to the sidewalk.*

*When kerosene was invented and the oil provided by the whaling industry was no longer needed, Nantucket was thrown into a deep depression that lasted for decades. Until tourism started, slowly, in the 1870s, the island's economic slump protected it from the influence of the mainland's Victorian styles, helping to make Nantucket what it is today: a town suspended in time.*

where her father—also an astronomer—worked as a cashier. One of 10 children, Mitchell was the first woman astronomy professor in the United States, and the first woman to discover a comet. The restored 1790 house contains family possessions and Maria Mitchell memorabilia, including the telescope with which she spotted the comet. The kitchen, of authentic wide-board construction, retains the antique utensils, iron pump, and sink of the time. Tours of the house and the roof walk are included in the admission price. The adjacent observatory is used by researchers and is not open to the public. *1 Vestal St., tel. 508/228–2896. $3 or MMA pass. Mid-June–mid-Sept., Tues.–Sat. 10–4.*

Built between 1829 and 1834, the handsome Federal brick house
3 known as **Moors' End** is where merchant Jared Coffin lived before moving to what is now the Jared Coffin House (☞ *above*)—the proximity to the fumes from the Starbuck refinery was one of Mrs. Coffin's complaints. It is a private home, so you won't be able to see Stanley Rowland's vast murals of the whaling era on the walls or the scrawled notes about shipwreck sightings in the cupola, but keep an eye out for pictures in any number of coffee-table books about Nantucket. Behind the home's high brick walls is the largest walled garden on Nantucket; like the house, it is not open to the public. *19 Pleasant St.*

A dozen historic Nantucket Town properties are operated as museums by the **Nantucket Historical Association (NHA).** At any one of them you can purchase an NHA Visitor Pass ($10 for adults, $5 for children 5–14), which entitles you to entry at all of the properties, or you can pay single admission at each (prices vary). You can also buy a pass at the association's **museum shop** (11 Broad St.), open April–December. Most sites are open daily from Memorial Day to Columbus Day. The Whaling Museum (☞ *below*) is open later in the season. *2 Whaler's La., tel. 508/228–1894.*

27 The **Nantucket Information Bureau** has public phones, rest rooms, maps, and a bulletin board posting special events. The staff (though it may be just one person manning the desk) gives

candid recommendations and can assist with reservations. This is the best place to turn to if you're tempted to extend your stay and need accommodations. 25 *Federal St., tel. 508/228–0925. July–Labor Day, daily; Labor Day–June, weekdays. Call for hrs.*

It's tough to escape the law when you live on an island. Those who
9 did not obey the rules and regulations ended up in the **Old Gaol,** an 1805 jailhouse in use until 1933. Shingles mask the building's construction of massive square timbers, plainly visible inside. Walls, ceilings, and floors are bolted with iron. The furnishings consist of rough plank bunks and open privies, but you needn't feel too much sympathy for the prisoners: most of them were allowed out at night to sleep in their own beds. 15R *Vestal St. Free. Memorial Day–Labor Day, daily 10–5; Labor Day–Columbus Day, daily 11–3.*

Several windmills sat on Nantucket hills in the 1700s, but only
2 the **Old Mill,** a 1746 Dutch-style octagonal windmill built with lumber from shipwrecks, remains. The Douglas-fir pivot pole used to turn the cap and sails into the wind is a replacement of the original pole, a ship's foremast. The mill's wooden gears work on wind power, and when the wind is strong enough, corn is ground into meal that is sold here. 50 *Prospect St., at S. Mill St., tel. 508/228–1894. $2 or NHA pass. Memorial Day–Labor Day, daily 10–5; Labor Day–Columbus Day, daily 11–3.*

History and architecture buffs should be sure to get a look at the
30 hilltop **Oldest House,** also called the Jethro Coffin House, built in 1686 as a wedding gift for Jethro and Mary Gardner Coffin. The most striking feature of the saltbox—the oldest house on the island—is the massive central brick chimney with brick horseshoe adornment. Other highlights are the enormous hearths and diamond-pane leaded-glass windows. Cutaway panels show 17th-century construction techniques. The interior's sparse furnishings include an antique loom. *Sunset Hill (a 10- to 15-min walk out Centre St. from Main St.), tel. 508/228–1894. $3 or NHA pass. Memorial Day–Columbus Day, daily 10–5; call for off-season hrs.*

19 The **Pacific Club** building still houses the elite club of Pacific whaling masters for which it's named. However, since the last whaling ship was seen here in 1870, the club now admits whalers' descendants, who gather for the odd cribbage game or a swapping of tales. The building first served in 1772 as the counting house of William Rotch, owner of the *Dartmouth* and *Beaver*, two of the three ships that hosted a famous tea party in Boston. According to the NHA, the plaque outside the Pacific Club identifying the third ship, the *Eleanor*, as Rotch's is incorrect. *Main and Federal Sts.*

18 Like the Pacific Club (☞ *above*) it faces, the 1818 **Pacific National Bank** is a monument to the far-flung voyages of the Nantucket whaling ships it financed. Inside, above old-style teller cages, are murals of street and port scenes from the whaling days. But this is no relic—the bank is still in use today. *61 Main St.*

★ 26 The **Peter Foulger Museum,** an exact replica of the Coffin School (☞ *above*) built in the 1970s, hosts engaging changing exhibits from the NHA's permanent collection, including portraits, historical documents, and furniture. The 2000 exhibit, "The Tragedy of the Whaleship *Essex*," included a captivating storytelling by a talented docent, who related what necessary horrors transpired when the *Essex* was struck by a whale and its crew were left to perish in the Pacific. "I have no language to point out the horrors of the situation," said First Mate Owen Chase rather famously. Fortunately he published his account in 1821, documenting the survival of the members of craft and confirming myths of their cannibalism. Chase's account would come to inspire a seaman named Herman Melville. *15 Broad St., tel. 508/228–1655. $5 or NHA pass. Memorial Day–mid-June and Columbus Day–Thanksgiving, weekends 11–3; mid-June–Labor Day, daily 10–5; Labor Day–Columbus Day, daily 11–3.*

20 Built around 1838 as a Friends school, the **Quaker Meeting House** is now a place of worship year-round. A small room of quiet simplicity, with antique-glass 12-over-12 windows and unadorned

## Petticoat Row

*During the whaling era—a time, remember, when women were generally considered better seen than heard—a circumstance developed in Nantucket Town that was perhaps unique in the country: a large portion of Centre Street shops near Main Street were almost completely run by women merchants. It eventually became known as Petticoat Row, and it still exists today.*

*Women have always played a strong role in Nantucket's history, partly because of the Quaker philosophy of sexual equality and partly because on whaling expeditions men could be gone for years at a time—and it was up to women to keep the town going. They became leaders in every arena, from religion to business. Mary Coffin Starbuck helped establish Quakerism on the island and was a celebrated preacher. Lucretia Coffin Mott became a powerful advocate for abolition and women's suffrage.*

*A 1999 survey showed that on Petticoat Row, at least, women still have the upper hand. Nearly half the businesses here are today run by women. They may no longer be selling grain or corsets, but they continue to uphold the island's proud tradition of matriarchal leadership.*

wood benches, it is in keeping with the Quaker tenets that the divine spirit is within each person and that no one requires an intermediary (or elaborate churches) to worship God. The unattractive adjoining 1904 concrete building is the **Fair Street Museum,** which presents rotating exhibits such as the NHA's collection of antique lightship baskets and portraits of historical Nantucket figures. *1 Fair St., tel. 508/636–3793. $3 or NHA pass. Services Wed. at 7 PM and Sun. at 10 AM.*

21 On a hot day, peek into the 1901 **St. Paul's Episcopal Church,** a massive granite structure adorned at the front and back by beautiful Tiffany windows. The interior is cool and white, with dark

exposed beams, and offers a quiet sanctuary from the crowds and the heat. *20 Fair St., tel. 508/228–0916. Services Sun. at 8* AM *and 10* AM.

Nantucket is packed with places that speak of its history. Off New Dollar Lane by Milk Street, and down a long driveway, the
5 remains of the **Starbuck refinery and candle works** are now used as apartments and garages.

Many of the mansions of the golden age of whaling were built
★ 12 on Upper Main Street. The well-known **"Three Bricks,"** identical redbrick mansions with columned, Greek Revival porches at their front entrances, were built between 1836 and 1838 by whaling merchant Joseph Starbuck for his three sons. One house still belongs to a Starbuck descendant. The Three Bricks are similar in design to the Jared Coffin House (☞ *above*) but have only two stories. They are not open to the public. *93–97 Upper Main St.*

22 The 1809 **Unitarian Universalist Church,** also known as South Church, has a gold-dome spire that soars above town, just as the First Congregational Church's (☞ *above*) slender white steeple does. Also like First Congregational, South Church has a trompe-l'oeil ceiling painting, this one simulating an intricately detailed dome and painted by an unknown European artist in 1840. Here, however, illusion is taken to greater lengths: the curved chancel and paneled walls you see are also creations in paint. The 1831 mahogany-cased Goodrich organ in the loft is played at services and concerts. In the octagonal belfry of the tower, which houses the town clock, is a bell cast in Portugal that has been ringing out the noon hour ever since it was hung in 1815. *11 Orange St., at Stone Alley, tel. 508/228–2730. Services Sun. at 10:45* AM.

At the **Vestal Street Observatory,** a tiny brick building built in 1908, daytime tours concentrate on the history and development of the telescope, and sunspot observations can be arranged. The museum also has an outdoor solar system model and an intricate sundial that is accurate almost to the minute. *3 Vestal St., tel. 508/*

*228–9273. $3 or NHA pass. Mid-June–mid-Sept., Tues.–Sat. tour at 11 AM; mid-Sept.–mid-June, Sat. tour at 11 AM.*

Immersing you in Nantucket's whaling past with exhibits that include a fully rigged whaleboat and a skeleton of a 43-ft finback
★ 25 whale, the **Whaling Museum,** set in an 1846 factory built for refining spermaceti and making candles, is a must-see. Also exhibited are harpoons and other whale-hunting implements; portraits of authentic sea captains; a large collection of scrimshaw; a full-size tryworks once used to process whale oil aboard ship; replicas of cooper, blacksmith, and other ship-fitting shops; and the original 16-ft-high lens from Sankaty Head Lighthouse. To help you contextualize all this paraphernalia, the knowledgeable and enthusiastic staff gives a 20- to 30-minute introductory talk peppered with tales of a whaler's life at sea (call for times). Don't miss the museum's gift shop next door. *13 Broad St., tel. 508/228–1894. $5 or NHA pass. Apr. and Columbus Day–Nov., weekends 11–3; May, daily 11–3; Memorial Day–Columbus Day, daily 10–5; Dec.–Mar., Sat. tour at 1:30.*

## SIASCONSET, POLPIS, AND WAUWINET

Siasconset began as a community of cod and halibut fishermen and shore whalers in the 17th century. But even then it was already becoming a summer resort as people from Nantucket Town 7 mi away would come here to get away from the smell of burning whale oil in the refineries. In 1884 the narrow-gauge railway—built three years earlier to take spiffily clad folk from the New Bedford steamers to the beach at Surfside—came to 'Sconset (as it's known locally) bringing ever more off-islanders. The writers and artists who came from Boston in the 1890s were soon followed by Broadway actors on holiday during the theaters' summer hiatus. Attracted by the village's beauty, remoteness, sandy ocean beach, and cheap lodgings—converted one-room fishing shacks, and cottages built to look like them—they spread the word, and before long 'Sconset became a thriving actors' colony.

# siasconset sightseeing

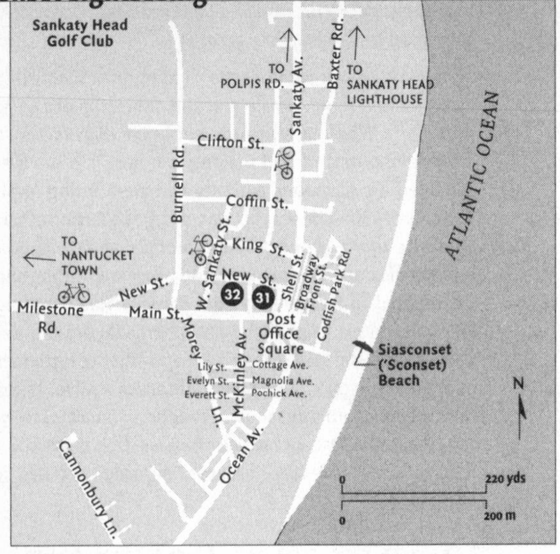


'Sconset Union Chapel, **32**

Siasconset Casino, **31**

Today a charming village of pretty streets with tiny rose-covered cottages and driveways of crushed white shells, 'Sconset is almost entirely a summer community. The local postmaster claims that about 150 families live here through the winter, but you'd never know it. At the central square are the post office, a market, and two restaurants, as well as a unique liquor store–cum–informal lending library. 'Sconset makes a lovely day trip from Nantucket Town—try it on bike, stopping to take a stroll in the village and continuing on to nearby beaches, bogs, and conservation areas.

*Numbers in the text correspond to numbers in the margin and on the Siasconset Sightseeing and Sightseeing Elsewhere maps.*

## A Good Tour: 'Sconset, Polpis, and Wauwinet

Start on foot with a stroll down three 'Sconset side streets—Evelyn, Lily, and Pochick, south of Main Street. (You'll eventually need your car or bike to complete this 12- to 15-mi tour.) These streets remain much as they were in the 1890s, when a development of tiny rental cottages in the fishing-shack style was built here. The summer blossoms of roses climbing all over many of the cottages weave fantastic carpets of color. From Pochick, turn left onto Ocean Avenue, passing 'Sconset Beach on your right (keep your eyes peeled for huge whale-shape topiaries), and walk north through Post Office Square to Broadway. Off Broadway Street is 'Sconset Pump—your Nantucket Nectar's cap will tell you it was "dug in 1776." From the pump, walk east on New Street toward **Siasconset Casino** ㉛—it's really a tennis club—and in summer take a peek at the beautiful entrance of Chanticleer (☞ Eating Out), the elegant French restaurant across the street. Just east on New Street are the **'Sconset Union Chapel** ㉜ and its pretty garden. From here hop in your car or on your bike and head north on Polpis Road, where hundreds of thousands of daffodils bloom in spring. A million Dutch bulbs were planted along Nantucket's main roads in 1974, and more have been planted every year since. Continue north on Polpis

## Nantucket Garden Club

*When some think of garden clubs, they may imagine idle, proper ladies in pillbox hats drinking tea—but not on Nantucket. "Here," says former Nantucket Garden Club president Nancy Seurens, "everybody works." And what beautiful work they've done—not only bringing to life the fragrant flowers bursting from every patch of yard and windowbox but also hosting three of the island's best-attended annual events. Two of these, the fund-raising House Tour and the Community Green Thumb Flower Show, have remained relatively low-key. But the third, Daffodil Weekend, has grown into an islandwide celebration signaling summer's arrival.*

*It all began in 1974 when member Jean MacAusland approached the club with the goal of planting a million daffodils. Islanders embraced the notion, and today fields of vibrant yellow line the roadsides. The big weekend, held in April, includes an antique and classic car parade, a picnic contest, and daffodil bouquets in every hand as Nantucket awakens after a long New England winter.*

Road past the striped **Sankaty Head Lighthouse** ㉝. The best place from which to see Sankaty Head is en route to or at **Sesachacha Pond** ㉞, which has a terrific view of the lighthouse and beyond. Then, continue northwest on Polpis for **Windswept Cranberry Bog** ㉟, the smaller of two island bogs. Just a mile or so west of the bog you'll come to the turnoff for **Wauwinet** ㊱ and **Coatue–Coskata–Great Point**—a terrific exploring area, worthy of a special trip. Continue east for the unmarked turnoff south to **Altar Rock** ㊲, the island's highest point, from which there's an incredible view of the surrounding moors, particularly at dawn or dusk. It's about a mile from Polpis Path. Return to Polpis Road, and continue west for a mile to Fulling Mill Road for the **Nantucket Life Saving Museum** ㊳, where artifacts recovered from the *Andrea Doria* are displayed. The museum is your last stop on the Polpis Path before Nantucket Town—just 3 mi left to go.

**TIMING**

Since the last stop on the tour closes at 4, try to get started early, touring 'Sconset and taking lunch here before visiting the sights off Polpis Road. This tour will take most of a day on bike and half a day by car. Note that there are no services in 'Sconset during the off-season.

## What to See

★ 37 An unmarked dirt track off Polpis Road between Wauwinet and Nantucket Town leads to **Altar Rock,** from which the view is spectacular. The rock sits on a high spot over open moor and bog land—technically called lowland heath—which is very rare in the United States. The entire area is laced with paths leading in every direction. Don't forget to keep track of the trails you travel in order to find your way back.

OFF THE BEATEN PATH ★ The **Milestone Bog,** more than 200 acres of working cranberry bogs surrounded by conservation land, is always a remarkably beautiful spot to visit, particularly at harvesttime (☞ Festivals *in* Practical Information). The harvest begins in late September and continues for six weeks, during which time harvesters work daily from sunup to sundown in flooded bogs. The sight of floating bright red berries and the moors' rich autumn colors is not to be missed. *Off Milestone Rd., west of Siasconset.*

38 In an interesting re-creation of an 1874 Life Saving Service station, the **Nantucket Life Saving Museum** displays items including original rescue equipment and boats, artifacts recovered from the wreck *Andrea Doria,* and photos and accounts of daring rescues. There are several rare pieces, for instance one of four existing surfboats, a mint-condition horse-drawn carriage from the Henry Ford Museum, and an equally well preserved original beach cart.

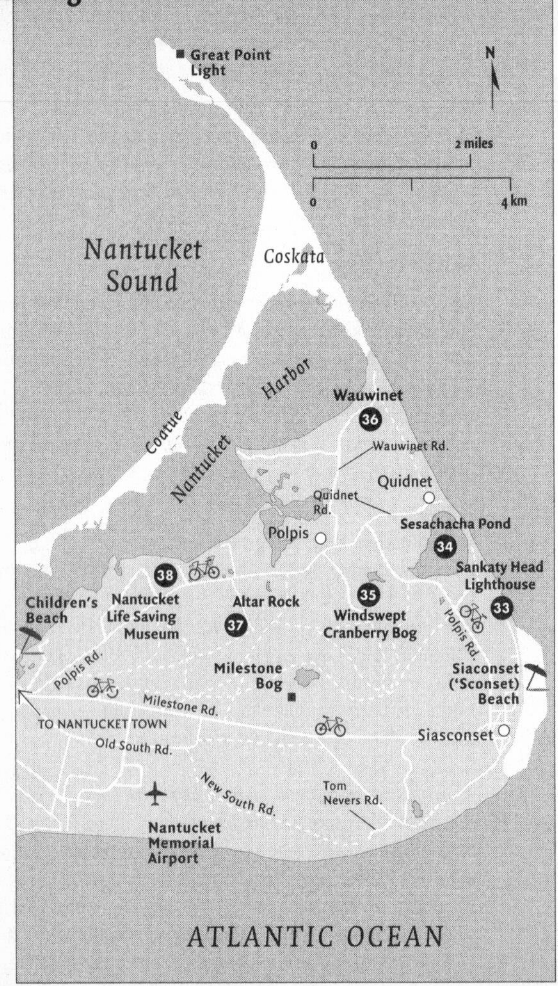
Great Point Light
N
0
2 miles
0
4 km
Nantucket Sound
Coskata
Harbor
Coatue
Nantucket
Wauwinet
36
Wauwinet Rd.
Quidnet
Quidnet Rd.
Polpis
Sesachacha Pond
34
Sankaty Head Lighthouse
33
38
Children's Beach
Nantucket Life Saving Museum
Altar Rock
37
35
Windswept Cranberry Bog
Polpis Rd.
Polpis Rd.
Milestone Bog
Siaconset ('Sconset) Beach
Milestone Rd.
TO NANTUCKET TOWN
Old South Rd.
Siasconset
New South Rd.
Tom Nevers Rd.
Nantucket Memorial Airport
ATLANTIC OCEAN

*158 Polpis Rd., 2½ mi east of Nantucket Town, tel. 508/228–1885. $3. Mid-June–Columbus Day, Tues.–Sun. 9:30–4.*

33 The red-and-white-stripe **Sankaty Head Lighthouse,** overlooking the sea on one side and the Scottish-looking links of the private Sankaty Head Golf Club (☞ Outdoor Activities and Sports) on the other, is one of New England's many endangered lighthouses. On a 90-ft-high bluff that has lost as much as 200 ft of shoreline in the past 75 years, the 1849 lighthouse could be lost, as Great Point Light was in 1984, to further erosion. Nantucket loses more of its shoreline every year, especially at Sankaty Head and on the south shore, where no shoals break the ocean waves as they do on the north shore. Some of that sand is simply moved along shore to the island's other end, but that's no great consolation to Sankaty Head and 'Sconset dwellers. The lighthouse is not open to the public, but you can approach it, via a seashell gravel road, for photos. *Off Polpis Rd.*

32 The **'Sconset Union Chapel,** the village's only church, holds Roman Catholic mass at 8:45 AM and Protestant services at 10:30 AM on summer Sundays. Even if you're not a churchgoer, it's worth a visit to see the almost 200 kneelers, individually designed by well-known needlepoint artist Erica Wilson, and the beautiful flower garden. *18 New St., tel. 508/257–6616.*

34 A good spot for bird-watching, **Sesachacha Pond** (pronounced, without all its syllables, as *sah*-kah-cha), off Polpis Road, is circled by a walking path that leads to an Audubon wildlife area. The pond is separated from the ocean by a narrow strand on its east side. From the pond, there's a good view of Sankaty Head Lighthouse (☞ *above*).

31 Despite its name, the 1899 **Siasconset Casino** has never been used for gambling—the meaning of "casino" was probably broader back when it was built—but was instead used from the beginning as a theater venue, particularly during the actors'-colony heyday, and as a gathering place. Some theater can still be seen here, but

it's primarily a tennis club and cinema. Though the clay-court tennis club is private, nonmembers can play between 1 and 3 during the summer (call first), provided they wear whites and tennis shoes and book on the same day. First-run movies are shown on Tuesday, Thursday, and Saturday in July and August. Opposite the casino is the much-photographed entryway of the Chanticleer restaurant (☞ Eating Out): a trellis arch topped by a sculpted hedge frames a rose garden with a flower-bedecked carousel horse at its center. *New St., tel. 508/257–6661.*

36 **Wauwinet** is a hamlet of beach houses on the northeastern end of Nantucket. European settlers found the neck of sand above it to be the easiest way to get to the ocean for fishing. Instead of rowing around Great Point, fishermen would go to the head of the harbor and haul their dories over the narrow strip of sand and beach grass separating Nantucket Harbor from the ocean. Hence the name for that strip: the haulover. Various storms have washed it out, allowing fishermen to sail clean through the area, but the shifting sands have continued to fill it back in.

In 1876 the Wauwinet House inn(☞ Eating Out *and* ☞ Where to Sleep) started luring townspeople to its 75¢ shore dinners. Local historian Jane Lamb, resident of a house called Chaos Corner on Wauwinet Road, relates the story of revelers who, on July 4, 1877, while sailing back to town after dancing until 11 PM, were grounded on shoals and rolled back and forth here until the tide rose with the sun. Happily, Wauwinet dinner cruises didn't die with that night, and you can still sail out to the inn for dinner.

35 Throughout the year, the 205-acre **Windswept Cranberry Bog** (off Polpis Rd.), part working bog, part conservation land, is a beautiful tapestry of greens, reds, and golds—and a popular hangout for many bird species. The bog is especially vibrant in mid-October, when the cranberries are harvested. (Although the weekend after Columbus Day has historically been a harvesting holiday, a glut in the market cancelled the harvesting in 2000. ☞ Call the Chamber of Commerce for information.) A map, as

## To the Lighthouse

*Probably since they were first invented—and one of the earliest was built in the 3rd century BC on the Pharos Peninsula at Alexandria—lighthouses have had a powerful pull on those who love the sea (or a good metaphor), standing tall in their unique architectural moment and guiding us home to familiar ground.*

*In Virginia Woolf's famous 1927 novel, the lighthouse represents both the unity and isolation one can feel as part of a family; the Ramsays focus on it as a sort of promised land, while recognizing that their individual visions of the structure separate them from one another. Today, the Great Point, Sankaty Head, and Brant Point lighthouses are among the most photographed and painted spots on Nantucket, an indelible part of the landscape, and an icon of island life. They link modern visitors to the men and women who first settled here, and there remains nothing quite so romantic as a lighthouse picnic of baguette, tapenade, and brie—just you and that special someone looking out to the vast blue of the sea.*

well as the 30-page "Handbook for Visitors to the Windswept Cranberry Bog," is available for $4 ($5 by mail) from the NCF (☞ Tours in Practical Information).

OFF THE BEATEN PATH **Coatue–Coskata–Great Point,** an unpopulated spit of sand comprising three cooperatively managed wildlife refuges, is a great place to spend a day relaxing or pursuing a favorite activity, such as bird-watching or fishing. **Coatue,** the strip of sand enclosing Nantucket Harbor, is open for many kinds of recreation—shellfishing for bay scallops, soft-shell clams, quahogs, and mussels (license required); surf casting for bluefish and striped bass (spring through fall); picnicking; or just enjoying the crowdless expanse. **Coskata**'s beaches,

dunes, salt marshes, and stands of oak and cedar attract marsh hawks, egrets, oystercatchers, terns, herring gulls, plovers, and many other birds, particularly during spring and fall migration. A successful program has brought ospreys here to nest on posts set up in a field by Coskata Pond. Don't come without field glasses.

Because of dangerous currents and riptides and the lack of lifeguards, swimming is strongly discouraged in the refuges, especially within 200 yards of the 70-ft stone tower of **Great Point Light.** Those currents, at the same time, are fascinating to watch at the Great Point tide rip. Seals and fishermen alike benefit from the unique feeding ground that it creates. The lighthouse is a 1986 re-creation of the light destroyed by a storm in 1984. The new light was built to withstand 20-ft waves and winds of up to 240 mph, and it was fitted with eight solar panels to power it.

You may only enter the area on foot or by four-wheel-drive vehicle, for which a permit is required ($85 for a year; $20 a day for a rental vehicle; tel. 508/228–2884). The permits are available at the **gatehouse at Wauwinet** (end of Wauwinet Rd., tel. 508/228–0006) June–September or off-season from a ranger patrolling the property. If you enter on foot, be aware that Great Point is a 5-mi walk from the entrance on soft, deep sand. Jeepless people often hitchhike here. Another alternative is a Jeep tour (☞ Tours in Practical Information).

*A group of 40 people hover before the India House Inn. Although the summer evening is warm, gooseflesh seems to be the dress code as Bill Jamieson of Nantucket Ghost Walk relates the macabre story of a green shimmering bubble that is said to haunt the old inn and restaurant. Although the building is not deserted, the front is dark and quiet, so it appears to be uninhabited. At the peak of the tension Mr. Jamieson so expertly builds with his story, the front door swings open. It's only a couple emerging from the restaurant, but it so startles the members of the group that one of them, a woman at the front, lets out a blood curdling scream. She, in turn, startles the hapless couple emerging from the building. Mr. Jamieson later admits it was the best tour he had given. "I wish I had three of that woman on every tour."*

## In This Chapter



*Revised and updated by Joyce Wagner*

# nightlife

**WHATEVER YOUR MUSICAL TASTES,** Nantucket's got you covered with a truly varied, albeit small, live-music scene. Reggae, funk, and alternative are common in pubs, plus many also have a DJ. So, if you're not entertained on your Nantucket vacation, well, you're just not trying. Other musical events, such as performances by the Boston Pops (☞ Music in Cultural Activities), and visits from big-name bands happen during summer. But, if you really want to see the stars, visit the Loines Observatory for astronomy lectures and telescope viewing. Of course, if it's just a beer you're after, you'll find that here, too.

## How and Where

The Straight Wharf (at the bottom of Main Street) is a bar-hoppers, haven, with several pubs tucked in among the T-shirt and souvenir shops. More venues are within walking distance on South Water, Federal, and Broad streets—just follow your ears for the spirited crowds and lively music. Several more can be found in outlying areas. The Muse, a large, noisy dance club with big-name bands, is near the airport, and the bar at the Bamboo Supper Club is off Pleasant Street. Most bars allow smoking, but there are enough open-air venues and smoke-free bars in which to have a good time if you don't indulge. Unless you've got a full head of hard-earned gray hair and a few age-appropriate worry lines, Nantucket bars are sticklers for IDs. Make sure you have yours with you. Bars close officially at 1:30 AM, although several close earlier. In the summer months, plan on standing in line at the more popular spots. Fortunately,

the happy, relaxed attitude of the crowds in queue can be as entertaining as the club itself.

## Sources

For listings of events, see the free weekly *Nantucket Map & Legend* (www.mapandlegend.com), the free year-round ferry-companion paper *Yesterday's Island* (www.yesterdaysisland.com), and the full-size island newspaper, the *Inquirer and Mirror* (www.ack.net). The Nantucket Web site www.yesterdaysisland.com posts an events calendar, with local music listings. Posters around town announce coming attractions, and be sure to check the board outside the Hub, a newsstand at the corner of Federal and Main streets.

# BARS AND CLUBS

The bar at the **Bamboo Supper Club** (3 Chins Way, tel. 508/228–0200), open till 1 AM, draws a young (21 to 30ish), zany crowd year-round. The club serves specialty drinks, such as "Scorpion Bowls" (rum, fruit punch, and Baccardi 151) and the instant buzz-making "Red Bull Purple Haze"—Chambord, Absolute Mandarin, and Red Bull over ice. The bartenders choose the music and they try to keep the atmosphere upbeat, crazy, and light. A pool table is upstairs.

**Bosuns Bistro** (14 Old South Wharf, tel. 508/228–7774), a seasonal breakfast and lunch spot, also has live jazz at night during summer.

The **Box** (16 Dave St., off Lower Orange St., tel. 508/228–9717), a.k.a. the Chicken Box, is open daily year-round and has live music six nights a week in season, and on weekends in the off-season. Lineups range from reggae to rock, and the cover charge depends upon the band. You can also play pool, Ping-Pong, and darts here.

**Brotherhood of Thieves** (23 Broad St., no phone) has live folk music year-round. The well-stocked bar has an interesting selection of beers and ales, plus dozens of cordials and liqueurs.

A major fire closed this place in mid-1999, but it's up and running with the same cool, quaint, and dark atmosphere.

The **Club Car Lounge** (Lower Main, tel. 508/228–1101) is open Memorial Day through the Christmas Stroll and has a lively piano bar. Requests and sing-alongs are encouraged, and you'll be crooning along with a mix of locals and visitors. If you're looking to make new friends, this is the joint.

The **Muse** (44 Surfside Rd., tel. 508/228–6873) is *the* place where big-name acts perform year-round. Some recent bands include Dave Matthews, Hootie and the Blowfish, and George Clinton. When there's no live act, people of all ages come here to dance to rock and reggae played by a DJ. It's typically a smoky, crowded place, holding more than 370 people on the dance floor and playing pool and Ping-Pong. The Muse also has a take-out pizza shop, **Muse Pizza** (tel. 508/228–1471; ☞ Eating Out).

**Rose and Crown** (23 S. Water St., tel. 508/228–2595) is a friendly, noisy, seasonal restaurant (open mid-April to October and Christmas Stroll weekend; ☞ Eating Out) with a big bar, a small dance floor, DJs, and theme nights, such as karaoke or toga parties.

The **Tap Room** (Jared Coffin House, 29 Broad St., tel. 508/228–2400; ☞ Eating Out), a favorite of locals, has been in business in the same historic building since 1847. Its quiet, intimate, 10-seat bar is great, casual place for a beer year-round until 11 PM.

The **Tavern and the Gazebo** (1 Harbor Sq., tel. 508/228–1266) are adjoining parking lots for "shopping widowers" by day, but at night they're quite a different animal. Under the same management, the Tavern (open May–Columbus Day) is slightly more subdued than its front-yard counterpart. The Gazebo (open May–mid-September) is the closest thing the island has to a singles bar. The 30-something crowd consists of an even mix of visitors and locals. The Tavern closes at 1 AM, the Gazebo at midnight.

## Maria Mitchell, Star Gazer

*On a clear night in 1847, a young woman peered through a telescope mounted on the roof of the Pacific Bank on Main Street. Although she had no formal training in astronomy, she had learned enough from her father, an amateur astronomer, to realize she was looking at a heretofore undiscovered comet. The young lady was Maria Mitchell, a native of Nantucket, who was later to become a fellow in the American Academy of Arts and Sciences and a teacher of astronomy at Vassar College. In 1970, the Maria Mitchell Association built the Loines Observatory to honor this island luminary. The observatory has a full-time, year-round astronomer on staff who gives lectures, and there are always several graduate students in residence who conduct tours and will cheerfully assist you and your family in adjusting the telescopes for a peek at the "Final Frontier." Who knows—maybe you'll discover a comet of your own.*

**Vincent's Upstairs Lounge** (21 S. Water St., tel. 508/228–0189) has live music on Wednesday and Thursday from 9 PM to 11:30 PM. Especially popular is the regular Thursday night band, a local jazz group called Big Unkie. A late-night pub menu is available after 10, and the room is smoke-free. It's open seasonally, from mid-May through October.

## OTHER DIVERSIONS

Peek through the big telescopes in two domes or the smaller ones set up on the deck of the **Loines Observatory** (59 Milk St., tel. 508/228–9273), one of several historic and scientific venues under the auspices of the Maria Mitchell Association (MMA; ☞ Here and There). Night viewing is on Monday, Wednesday, and

Friday at 9 PM in July and August, Wednesday at 8 PM the rest of the year—of course, it's always subject to the weather. Sometimes the observatory will add extra nights to the schedule. Admission is $10 for adults; $5 for MMA members.

Tour haunted island sites (including a cemetery) on the **Nantucket Ghost Walk** (Federal and India Sts., in front of the Atheneum, tel. 508/325–8855) at 7 PM Wednesday and Friday in June and nightly in July and August. Be there, if you dare!

*In just one summer month a Nantucket resident reported singing with a touring Gilbert & Sullivan company (she got to attend the fancy reception in flouncy period garb), participating in the reading of a world-premiere play, attending readings by fledgling and well-known authors, and taking in several top-notch concerts. Nantucket's cultural endeavors are anything but rinky-dink. Not only does the populace provide an unusually sophisticated audience, it comprises artists and performers of every conceivable stripe, which makes for never a dull weekend—even amid the doldrums of winter.*

## In This Chapter



*Revised and updated by Sandy MacDonald*

# cultural activities and events

**INTELLECTUAL CURIOSITY IS AS ALIVE TODAY ON NANTUCKET** as it was in the mid-18th century, when citizens flocked to the Atheneum's Great Hall to hear such speakers as Melville, Emerson, and Thoreau. Today the roster runs to Paul Theroux, Anna Quindlan, and other nationally known names. Nantucket supports two non-Equity theater companies—"amateur" in the best sense—which can be counted on for gripping performances. While plans percolate for a permanent performing arts center, plays often go up in a handful of church halls, which may also host concerts. On Friday evenings in summer, a scattering of art galleries (☞ Shopping) hold their openings, and you can wander from one to the next, feasting on the art and complimentary canapes. As for cinema, Nantucket has three—Dreamland Theatre, Gaslight, and Siasconset Casino, covering Hollywood's latest blockbusters as well as independents.

## Sources

For listings of events, see the two free tabloid-size weeklies, the *Nantucket Map & Legend* (www.mapandlegend.com) and *Yesterday's Island* (www.yesterdaysisland.com), both widely distributed year-round, and the regular island newspaper, the *Inquirer and Mirror*, whose Web site (www.ack.net)—named for the island's airport code—lists events. Posters around town announce coming attractions, and be sure to check the board

outside the Hub, a newsstand at the corner of Federal and Main streets.

## CLUBS AND CLASSES

The **Nantucket Garden Club** (Point Breeze Hotel, 17 Easton St., tel. 508/228–2702), a members-only summer club, puts on dazzling shows at the Point Breeze Hotel.

The **Nantucket Community School** (Nantucket High School, 10 Surfside Rd., tel. 508/228–7257) offers a wide range of courses year-round, from dog obedience to meditation; some qualify for college credit.

## FILM AND PHOTOGRAPHY

In June, the Dreamland and Gaslight theaters host the films associated with the Nantucket Film Festival (☞ *below*). Theaters in Nantucket don't seem to mind if you bring in outside food and drink.

The **Dreamland Theater** (17 S. Water St., tel. 508/228–5356) is housed in a pleasant ramshackle old ark of a building, which used to be a Quaker meetinghouse, then a straw factory, and, finally, an entertainment hall. It's now a summer cinema (open mid-May–mid-September) running two shows nightly of first-run mainstream movies and the occasional rainy-day matinee.

The **Gaslight Theater** (1 N. Union St., tel. 508/228–4435), a small screening room appended to the White Dog Cafe (☞ Eating Out), shows mostly foreign, art, and independent films. The schedule can be iffy, but there are usually two shows nightly, plus sporadic matinees and midnight screenings.

The **Nantucket Film Festival** (tel. 508/325–6274 or 212/642–6339, www.nantucketfilmfestival.org), a popular island event garnering celebrity turnout, is held annually in mid-June, with film screenings, staged readings, panel discussions, informal moderated discussions, and plenty of parties.

## Nantucket Film Festival

*With the tagline "Where screenwriters inherit the earth," the Nantucket Film Festival (www.nantucketfilmfestival.com) emphasizes the importance of strong scripts—a criterion that also informs the juried selection from hundreds of international submissions. The final playlist—about two dozen short and feature-length films—always includes a few world premieres, and many selections, like* The Full Monty, *go on to considerable commercial success. Tickets go on sale 15 minutes before showtime. Weeklong passes (upwards of $300), though pricy, let you cut the inevitable lines. Daily passes ($50) are also recommended if you intend to attend more than one screening. Informal daily coffee-klatch events, such as close-up discussions with directors held at local restaurants, are less costly ($5) and can also be interesting. Throughout the festival, you can cast your vote for the best feature and the best short feature. The winners are announced at the closing-night party.*

The **Nantucket Slide Film** (Nantucket United Methodist Church, 2 Centre St., tel. 508/228–3783), presented Monday–Saturday evenings throughout the summer, showcases annual highlights by island photographer Cary Hazelgrove.

The **Siasconset Casino** (New St., Siasconset, tel. 508/257–6661), a 100-year-old hall, has nothing to do with gambling: at the turn of the 20th century, the term merely meant a place to gather for entertainment. First-run movies are shown, auditorium-style, Tuesday, Thursday, and Sunday evenings at 8:30, June through Labor Day. Old hands know to bring pillows. Admission is $5.

## FINE ARTS AND CRAFTS

The **Artists Association of Nantucket** (Gardner Perry La., tel. 508/228–0722), founded in 1945, offers classes year-round in various media, often led by some of the island's most noteworthy artists. The association's **gallery** (19 Washington St., tel. 508/228–0294) hosts shows and occasional special events.

The **Lightship Shop** (20 Miacomet Ave., tel. 508/228–4164) offers lightship basket-making classes in summer. A three-day course is about $350.

**Milestone Art** (69 Milestone Rd., tel. 508/228–9662) is Dee Macy's gallery and studio, where she offers private and group instruction in painting.

The **Nantucket Island School of Design and the Arts** (23 Wauwinet Rd., tel. 508/228–9248, www.nantucket.net/art/nisda), affiliated with the Massachusetts College of Art in Boston, has year-round art classes for all ages in virtually all media, as well as lectures and shows.

**Shredder's Studio** (3 Salros Rd., tel. 508/228–4487) has more than a dozen art classes for various ages (children and up) in assorted media.

**Sketching Tours of Nantucket** (tel. 508/228–1478) consists of small groups led by artist Anne Baldwin Butler to prize doorways, gates, and gardens.

## HISTORICAL TOURS

Walking tours generally cover the major sights within the historic district; motor tours in air-conditioned buses typically make a loop through 'Sconset. The tour operators listed below won't make you feel like a tourist or rip you off like one.

The **Friends of the African Meeting House** (York and Pleasant Sts., tel. 508/228–8933; ☞ Here and There) leads a "Walk the Black Heritage Trail" tour twice a week in season.

**Gail's Tours** (tel. 508/257–6557) are van excursions led by Gail Nickerson Johnson, an ebullient seventh-generation native.

The **Nantucket Ghost Walk** (Atheneum, 1 India St., tel. 508/325–8855) departs every night July–August at 7 PM from the steps of the Atheneum.

The **Nantucket Historical Association** (Whaling Museum, 15 Broad St., tel. 508/325–1894, www.nha.org) sponsors twice-daily—except Sunday—docent-led walking tours in season from the Whaling Museum, at about half the going rate.

**Walking Tours with Dirk Gardiner Roggeveen** (tel. 508/221–0075), who is a 12th-generation islander, runs 1½–2 lore-packed hours, every afternoon except Sunday, from May to mid-October and at other times by appointment; children tag along free.

## LITERARY GROUPS AND ACTIVITIES

**Linear Arts** (24 Amelia Dr., tel. 508/825–9153), a bookstore–slash–literary salon, hosts readings by neophytes and professionals alike and affordable workshops in various genres; events vary week to week, so call for a schedule. Linear Arts also publishes a magazine, *Nantucket Writings.*

The **Nantucket Atheneum** (1 India St., tel. 508/228–1110) holds free monthly meetings for poets of all levels.

## KIDS' STUFF

Most of these organizations have supervised evening, short-term, or summer programs for children. For more ideas on what to do with your youngsters or for events you and your children can do together, *see* Outdoor Activities and Sports.

The **Children's Theatre of Nantucket** (Nantucket High School, 10 Surfside Rd., tel. 508/228–7257, ext. 1576) takes over the 600-seat auditorium of the Nantucket High School for weekly productions in summer.

The **Maria Mitchell Association** (various venues, tel. 508/228–9198 association office; ☞ Here and There) organizes various nature-centered activities for age groups 4–11.

**Murray Camp** (25½ Bartlett Rd., tel. 508/325–4600) is a venerable day program for ages 5–14, available by the week or season late June–mid-August. It has all the usual camp offerings (swimming, sailing, etc.), plus electives such as "Fun French" plus "Kids' Nights Out" and family evenings.

The **Nantucket Atheneum** (1 India St., tel. 508/228–1110) holds regular storytelling and book-club meetings for various ages.

The **Nantucket Boys & Girls Club** (61 Sparks St., tel. 508/228–0158), part of the national organization, has a spacious modern facility where recreational and educational after-school, weekend, and vacation-time programs are held year-round.

The **Nantucket Community Music Center** (11 Centre St., tel. 508/228–5422) runs a band camp culminating in a performance at the Children's Beach bandstand.

The **Nantucket Historical Association** (15 Broad St., tel. 508/228–1894, www.nha.org) sponsors special hands-on living-history programs for ages 6–10.

**Nantucket.net** (2 Union St., tel. 508/228–5234) hosts "Kids Night at the InterNet"—three hours of supervised games and surfing—on Friday and Saturday nights in summer for ages 8–14.

The **Nantucket Park & Recreation Commission** (tel. 508/228–7213) offers free puppet shows, arts-and-crafts programs, and family concerts at Children's Beach in season. It also maintains a bring-your-own-equipment skateboarding and blading park near the public tennis courts at Jetties Beach; tennis clinics are available for ages 4–14.

**Strong Wings Adventure School** (tel. 508/228–1769, www.strongwings.org) has courses for children 5–16, including kayaking and mountain-biking.

The **Teen Center** (First Way, tel. 508/325–5435), open Friday and Saturday nights year-round, offers activities and just a place to hang out.

The **Toy Boat** (Straight Wharf, tel. 508/228–4552, www.thetoyboat.com) offers a summer schedule of fun and educational activities, all of which are free.

## MUSIC

Many concerts are free or reasonably priced at $10–$20. Benefits can ascend into three figures.

The **Boston Pops Esplanade Orchestra** (tel. 508/825–8248) puts on a blow-out concert in late July on Jetties Beach to benefit the Nantucket Cottage Hospital.

The **Cross Rip Coffee House** (Nantucket United Methodist Church, 3 Centre St., tel. 508/228–4352) brings jazz and folk singer-songwriters, both established and up-and-comers, to the island off-season.

**Nantucket Arts Council** (Coffin School, 4 Winter St., tel. 508/228–2190) sponsors a music series (jazz, country, classical) September to June.

The **Nantucket Community Music Center** (11 Centre St., tel. 508/228–5422 or 508/228–3352) not only arranges year-round choral and instrumental instruction but sponsors and puts on concerts; choristers are always welcome.

The **Nantucket Multi-cultural Council** (tel. 508/325–5003) sponsors a Community Drum Circle at the Children's Beach bandstand off Harbor View Way Wednesday evenings in summer.

**Nantucket Musical Arts Society** (First Congregational Church, 62 Centre St., tel. 508/228–1287) mounts concerts by internationally acclaimed musicians Tuesday evenings at 8:30 July–August and has done so since 1959. The concerts are mostly classical, but the group has occasionally ventured into jazz.

The **Nantucket Park & Recreation Commission** (Children's Beach bandstand, off Harbor View Way, tel. 508/228–7213) hosts free concerts (and the occasional theater production) from July 4 to Labor Day. Programs begin at 6 PM, range from jazz and classical to pop, and include such local favorites as Ecliff & the Swingdogs. Bring blankets, chairs, and bug repellent.

The **Noonday Concert Series** (11 Orange St., tel. 508/228–5466), Thursday at noon in July and August, brings in stellar performers and also showcases outstanding local musicians. Past concerts have included organ, bluegrass, and classical music.

## READINGS AND TALKS

The **Coffin School** (4 Winter St., tel. 508/228–2505) is the site of lectures (some sponsored by the resident Egan Institute for Maritime Studies), as well as occasional concerts.

The **Nantucket Atheneum** (1 India St., tel. 508/228–1110) hosts a dazzling roster of writers and speakers year-round. Except for a few big-name fundraisers in summer, all events are free.

The **Nantucket Cottage Hospital** (57 Prospect St., tel. 508/228–1200) sponsors occasional lectures on health topics of general interest, such as—alas—Lyme disease.

The **Nantucket Historical Association** (15 Broad St., tel. 508/228–1894 www.nha.org; ☞ Here and There) hosts evening talks on a variety of topics touching on local history.

## THEATER

**Actors Theatre of Nantucket** (Nantucket United Methodist Church, 2 Centre St., tel. 508/228–6325, www.nantuckettheatre.com) mounts a half-dozen professional productions in an intimate basement space Memorial Day–Columbus Day, plus children's matinees, comedy nights, and occasional improv and readings. In the off-season, the theater becomes the Cross-Rip Coffeehouse.

**Theatre Workshop of Nantucket** (Bennett Hall, 62 Centre St., tel. 508/228–4305, www.theatreworkshop.com), a community theater since 1956, stages plays, musicals, and readings year-round.

## TV AND RADIO

**Nantucket Television–Channel 22** (Pacific Club, 15 Main St., tel. 508/228–8001), the island's community-access cable channel, is considered must-viewing by many. Several islanders, such as independent filmmaker Geno Geng and grande dame Martha Walters, have their own shows with a devoted following.

**WNAN 91.1** (tel. 508/548–9600, www.cainan.org) is Nantucket's own NPR station, a thrilling millennial addition to the island's cultural discourse. Interspersed amid the standard NPR fare are local vignettes and coverage of island-specific issues.

*The phone is ringing, and there is someone at the door with an inquiry. But the proprietor of this Chestnut Street guesthouse answers the door with a big smile. "Hang on just a minute," she says before grabbing the phone. After giving detailed directions and answering a number of questions involving the weather, distance to beaches, and room amenities, she turns to her visitor with cheerful demeanor and asks how she can help. "How do you stay so cheerful in August?" the visitor wants to know, and the innkeeper's response is immediate: "This is Nantucket," she says simply, again beaming that radiant smile. Like their guests, innkeepers are, quite obviously, happy to be here.*

## In This Chapter



*Revised and updated by Debi Stetson*

# where to stay

**FROM SMALL BED & BREAKFASTS TO THE ISLAND'S LARGEST 100-ROOM HOTEL,** Nantucket knows hospitality. And good service, as busy as this little island is, keeps visitors coming back year after year. Reservations are a must and should be made well in advance, especially if you'll be visiting in the busy summer season. Nantucket has only 1,200 beds available at any given time, and in summer, as many as 40,000 people visit per day. Many places require a minimum stay of three nights in summer and have strict cancellation policies. If you're on the island and having trouble finding accommodations, Nantucket Visitor Services tracks cancellations daily and can direct you to newly available rooms—but it does not make reservations for you.

Apart from cottages and a few inns and hotels scattered across the island, most lodgings are in Nantucket Town, convenient to shops and restaurants—in season there may be some evening street noise. Inns just outside the town center, a 5- or 10-minute walk from Main Street, are quieter. Many of the smaller inns are furnished with antiques and cannot accommodate children; families should consider the larger inns, especially those that offer separate cottages, such as the Harbor House, White Elephant, and Point Breeze Hotel.

Meal services vary greatly, even among inns. Some provide coffee in common rooms, some deliver breakfast to your room, and others offer vouchers to nearby restaurants. If appliances such as coffeemakers and mini-refrigerators are important to your stay, ask about them when you reserve a room. Some inns have air-conditioning, but many do not—as innkeepers will tell you, it's usually not an issue even on hot summer days, because of the cool ocean breezes. An increasing number of inns are smoke-free, so be sure to ask about the policy if you indulge.

| CATEGORY | COST* |
|---|---|
| **$$$$** | over $200 |
| **$$$** | $150–$200 |
| **$$** | $100–$150 |
| **$** | under $100 |

**All prices are for a standard double room, in high season excluding 4% Nantucket and 5.7% state taxes.*

## Prices

Nantucket is notoriously expensive, so don't look for bargains in lodging, at least not in summer. The best rates can be found in the off-season, but the spring and fall "shoulder" seasons have become quite popular, too, and such special-event weekends as the Daffodil Festival in April and Christmas Stroll in December inspire summer rates. Most inns charge between $150 and $185 a night in summer, but many go higher. On the upper extreme is the Wauwinet, which charges from $540 to $1,000 a night, and the new two-bedroom cottages at the White Elephant get $1,000 a night. Although many islanders shook their heads at these prices, the cottages were booked solid their first season. The only inexpensive facility you'll find is the Star of the Sea Youth Hostel, which is the only option for roughing it, as camping is not allowed anywhere on the island. Besides, Nantucket is really not about roughing it; this island is all charm and comfort. Plan to splurge here—on everything. We list months closed; otherwise it's safe to assume that places are open year-round.

## NANTUCKET TOWN LODGING

**$$$$** **CLIFFSIDE BEACH CLUB.** Once you've gotten here, you may not be inclined to leave—enjoying the beach may be occupation enough. Although the cedar-shingle exterior, landscaped with climbing roses and hydrangeas, and the pavilion on the private sandy beach 1 mi from town reflect the club's 1920s origins, the interiors are done in contemporary summer style, with white walls, white or natural wood furniture, cathedral ceilings, and local art. Some have fireplaces, wet bars, or private decks. Two large "town-house suites" have full kitchens and decks overlooking dunes, moors, and Nantucket Sound. Front rooms are reserved for adults only; children are welcome in the apartments. *46 Jefferson Ave., Box 449, 02554, tel. 508/228–0618, fax 508/325–4735. 26 rooms, 3 suites, 2 apartments, 1 cottage. Restaurant, piano bar, kitchenettes (some), exercise room, beach, playground. AE. Closed mid-Oct.–May. CP. www.nantucketislandresorts.com*

**$$$$ HARBOR HOUSE.** Although a bit on the corporate side, Harbor House, is one of those everything-in-its-place resorts. It may lack the character of a small B&B, but it's open year-round and has such comfort-enhancing extras as sofa beds and off-room decks, cable TV, phones, and summer children's activities. Plus, upon request a shuttle will pick you up from the Steamship ferry. Standard rooms are done in English-country style. Some have French doors that open onto decks. The generally larger town-house rooms, in buildings grouped around the pool, have a more traditional look. Some have cathedral ceilings. The private cottage has its own garden, but its rooms are smaller. Brick walkways connect the main inn, which dates to 1886, with the town houses, thereby creating a community feel to this well-run complex. Owned by Steven Karp, who also owns the posh Wauwinet, the White Elephant, and the Breakers Inn, Harbor House is now part of Nantucket Island Resorts. Its restaurant, the Food Fare at the Harbor House, is an island favorite with a lovely outdoor patio—great for families with hungry children in tow. *South Beach St., Box 1139, 02554, tel. 508/228–1500; 800/475–2637 for reservations; fax 508/228–7639. 109 rooms. Restaurant, lounge, pool, children's programs*

# nantucket town lodging

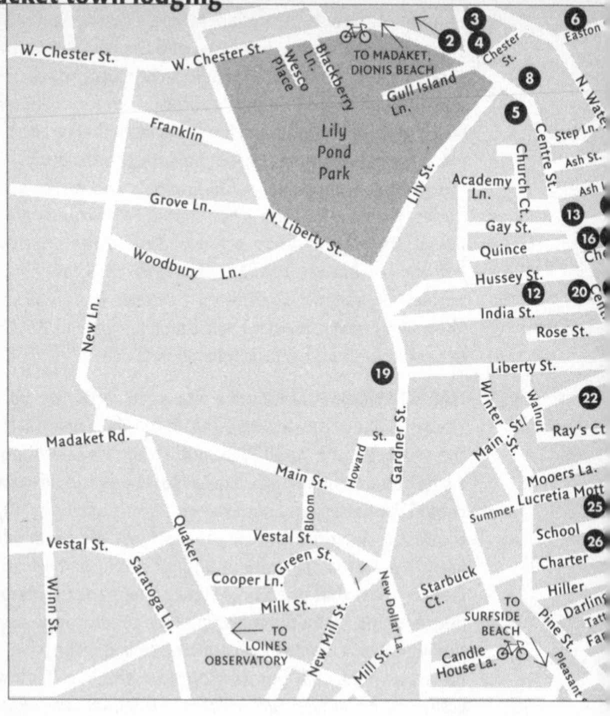


Anchor Inn, **5**
Beachside at Nantucket, **1**
Centerboard Guest House, **4**
Century House, **3**
Chestnut House, **17**
Cliff Lodge, **2**
18 Gardner Street, **19**
The Grey Lady, **20**
Harbor House, **9**
Hawthorn House, **18**
Jared Coffin House, **13**
Lyon Street Inn, **27**
Manor House, **16**
Martin House Inn, **8**
Nantucket Whaler Guest House, **15**
Nesbitt Inn, **14**
Pineapple Inn, **12**
Point Breeze Hotel, **6**
Roberts House Inn, **21**
Safe Harbot, **10**
Seven Sea Street, **12**
76 Main Street, **22**
Ships Inn, **25**

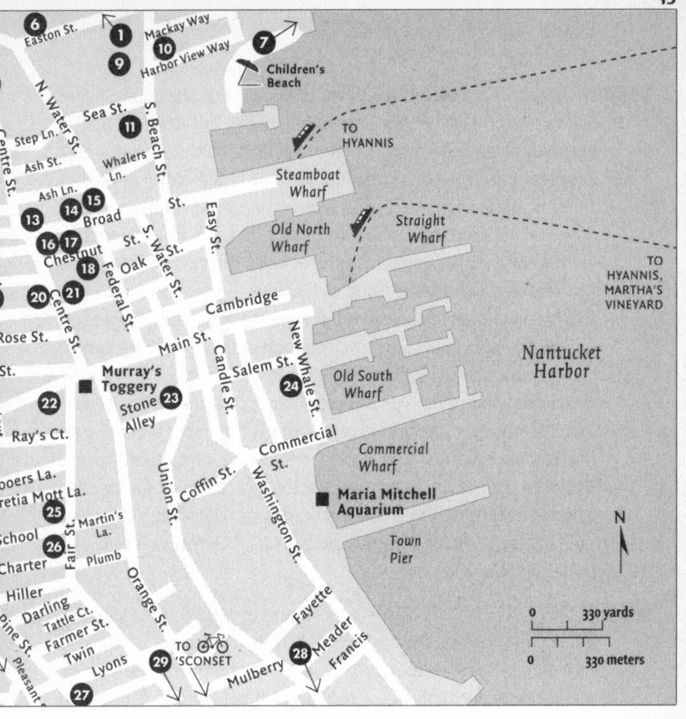

Easton St.
Mackay Way
Harbor View Way
Children's Beach
N. Water St.
Sea St.
S. Beach St.
Step Ln.
Centre St.
Ash St.
Whalers Ln.
TO HYANNIS
Steamboat Wharf
Ash Ln.
Broad St.
Easy St.
Old North Wharf
Straight Wharf
Chestnut St.
S. Water St.
Oak St.
Federal St.
TO HYANNIS, MARTHA'S VINEYARD
Cambridge
Rose St.
Main St.
New Whale St.
Nantucket Harbor
Murray's Toggery
Candle St.
Salem St.
Old South Wharf
Stone Alley
Ray's Ct.
Commercial St.
Commercial Wharf
Union St.
Coffin St.
Washington St.
Maria Mitchell Aquarium
Martin's La.
School
Fair St.
Town Pier
N
Charter
Plumb
Hiller
Orange St.
Fayette
Darling
Tattle Ct.
Pine St.
Farmer St.
Meader
330 yards
Twin
TO 'SCONSET
Francis
330 meters
Pleasant
Lyons
Mulberry

*(ages 5–13), concierge, business services. AE, D, DC, MC, V. CP. www.nantucketislandresorts.com*

**$$$$ ★ NANTUCKET WHALER GUEST HOUSE.** The beautiful handpainted mural that covers the foyer and climbs with a floral border up the stairway is an indication of the attention to detail given this property. Don't let the name fool you—this isn't any run-of-the-mill inn. The level of luxury, special touches, and in-room amenities is unlike that of other guest houses, which, even here on Nantucket, are typically not quite so thoughtful or fancy. Built in 1850, the guest house was purchased in 2000 by Calliope Ligelis and Randi Ott, two hardworking mothers who have spent a great deal of time and energy transforming the place into such a classy inn. Fine linens, down comforters, plush robes, and towels for your trip to the beach are some of the extras you can expect. Each suite has its own entrance, deck, a kitchenette with mini-refrigerator, wet bar, and kitchen accessories, and both a microwave and toaster oven. Children over 12 are accepted, but this place is best for couples seeking a real getaway. *8 N. Water St., 02554, tel. 508/228–6597, fax 508-228-6291. 10 suites. Kitchenetts. AE, MC, V. Closed Dec. 15–Apr. 15. www.nantucketwhaler.com*

**$$$$ POINT BREEZE HOTEL.** This large, rambling old building maintains its elegant, turn-of-the-20th-century resort ambience, enhanced by a complete renovation by the Gonnella family, who purchased the property, formerly called the Folger Hotel, in 1998. Those who knew it before should definitely revisit and experience this once-again-grand Victorian hotel. The guest rooms and spacious common areas are airy and polished the gardens lush and well tended; the large, old-fashioned veranda relaxing and, on fine days, great for enjoying the sumptuous full breakfasts that are standard morning fare. In addition to rooms and suites in the main building, there are several adjacent cottages, with either two or four bedrooms. All rooms have cable TV. It's a short walk to town, Brant Point Lighthouse, and Children's Beach. Children are welcome; cribs are available upon advance request. *71 Easton St., 02554, tel. 508/228–*

*0313 or 800/365–4371, fax 508–325–6044. 8 rooms, 14 suites, 7 cottages. Restaurant, kitchenettes (some), room service, in-room data ports, airport shuttle. AE, MC, V. Closed mid-Oct.–mid-May. BP. www.pointbreeze.com*

**$$$$** **WHARF COTTAGES.** These weathered-shingle cottages sit on a wharf in Nantucket Harbor, with yachts moored just steps away—in fact, with reservations, you could arrive by boat and tie up at the marina. Each one has a little garden and sitting area, a fully equipped kitchen, and attractive modern decor with a nautical flavor: white walls, navy blue rugs, and light-wood floors and furniture. Studios have a sofa bed for sleeping. Other cottages have one to three bedrooms. All have water views, though they're not always equal—some cottages have extralarge windows. All of the amenities available at the Harbor House (☞ *above*) extend here, including the children's programs. *New Whale St., Box 1139, 02554, tel. 508/228–4620 or 800/475–2637, fax 508/228–7639. 25 cottages. Kitchenettes, dock. AE, D, DC, MC, V. Closed mid-Oct.–late Apr. BP.*

**$$$$** **WHITE ELEPHANT.** Completely redone in 1999 following its merger with the Harbor House (☞ *above*), the White Elephant has never looked better. Rooms and common areas are elegantly done, with a fresh, floral, white-wicker atmosphere. Its unbeatable location, right on Nantucket Harbor and bordered by a wide lawn and a cozy beach, is just a brief walk from town. From the wraparound deck of the main hotel or the formal Brant Point Grill (☞ Eating Out) with a waterside outdoor café, you'll have a fine view of the bobbing boats. A collection of new and refurbished garden cottages, all named for flowers and connected by landscaped walkways, is ideal for families. *Easton St., Box 1139, 02554, tel. 508/228–2500; 800/475–2637 for reservations; fax 508/325–1195. 24 rooms, 30 suites, 12 cottages. Restaurant, lounge, room service, putting green, dock, concierge, meeting rooms. AE, D, DC, MC, V. Closed late Oct.–mid-May. BP. www.whiteelephanthotel.com*

**$$$–$$$$** **BEACHSIDE AT NANTUCKET.** Those who prefer rooms-around-a-pool motels with all the creature comforts will find a very nice one here, though it's a bit of a walk from the town center. Each room in the one- and two-story buildings is furnished in wicker and florals and has a queen-size or two double beds, a tile bath, and a small refrigerator and coffeemaker. Some rooms have French doors opening onto pool-view decks. Public tennis courts are adjacent. *30 N. Beach St., 02554, tel. 508/228–2241 or 800/322–4433, fax 508/228–8901. 90 rooms, 3 2-bedroom suites. Pool, meeting rooms. AE, D, DC, MC, V. Closed mid-Oct.–mid-Apr. CP.*

**$$$–$$$$** ★ **CENTERBOARD GUEST HOUSE.** The look and polish of this no-smoking inn help differentiate it from any other Nantucket property. White walls, some with murals of moors and sky in soft pastels; blond-wood floors; and natural woodwork create a cool, dreamy atmosphere. There is yet more white in the lacy linens and puffy comforters on the feather beds. Touches of color are added by stained-glass lamps, antique quilts, and fresh flowers. The first-floor suite (right off the entry hall) is stunning, with 11-ft ceilings, a Victorian living room with fireplace and bar, inlaid parquet floors, and a green-marble bath with whirlpool bath. This island of calm isn't isolated, however; it's just a few blocks from the center of town. For those who need to stay in touch, even on vacation, each room has cable TV and phone. *8 Chester St., Box 456, 02554, tel. 508/228–9696. 6 rooms, 1 suite. Air-conditioning. AE, MC, V. CP. www.nantucket.net/lodging/centerboard*

**$$$–$$$$** **IVY LODGE.** This unpretentious inn is refreshingly free of in-room telephones and TVs, as European-born innkeeper Tuge Koseatac feels people need to get away from those things in order to truly relax. Built in 1790, this historic structure was run as a guest house and museum in the 1800s. Today's rooms are simple and old-fashioned, with Oriental carpets and brass or canopy beds. A Continental breakfast is served in the Great Room, in which you'll find the house's original fireplace with beehive oven, or on the garden patio, added in 2000. There is no smoking, and the lodge cannot accommodate children. *2 Chester St., 02554, tel. 508/228–*

*7755, fax 508/228–0305. 6 rooms, 1 suite. MC, V. Closed Dec.–Apr. CP. www.nantucket.net/lodging/ivy.*

**$$$–$$$$** ★ **JARED COFFIN HOUSE.** One of the most recognizable names on the island, this classic Nantucket property right in town was built by whaling captain Jared Coffin for his wife. The mansion—the main portion of this six-building hotel—was the first three-story brick structure built on Nantucket, a big news item in 1845. A hotel for more than a century, the year-round Jared Coffin House has wonderful historic ambience, especially in the main inn, which is furnished with antiques, Oriental carpets, and lace curtains. The Harrison Gray House, an 1842 Greek Revival mansion across the street, has larger guest rooms with large baths and queen-size canopy beds. Two newer buildings are close by on Centre Street, but they don't have the historical appeal of these two buildings. All rooms have phones and cable TV. Small, inexpensive single rooms are available. Breakfast is an event here, attracting not only off-island visitors but local businesspeople and residents as well. There are two choices for in-house dining. One is the more formal Jared's (☞ Eating Out), which serves classic dishes enhanced by an expansive wine list. (Dinner is not served January–April.) Downstairs, the less expensive Tap Room (☞ Eating Out *and* Nightlife), open year-round, is dark and cozy, with lots of exposed wood and nautical art and a comfortable bar serving pub fare. *29 Broad St., Box 1580, 02554, tel. 508/228–2400 or 800/248–2405, fax 508/228–8549. 60 rooms. Restaurant, bar, café, concierge. AE, D, DC, MC, V. BP. www.jaredcoffinhouse.com*

**$$$–$$$$** **LYON STREET INN.** Ann Marie and Barry Foster have combined an enthusiasm for history and an eye for detail to create a truly unique guest house. Their inn has been rebuilt with historical touches such as variable-width plank floors, salvaged Colonial mantels on the fireplaces, and hefty ceiling beams of antique red oak. The white walls and blond woodwork provide a clean stage for antique Oriental rugs in deep, rich colors; choice antiques, such as Room No. 1's French tester bed draped in white mosquito netting; and English floral fabrics, down comforters, and big pillows. Bathrooms are white and bright. Several have separate showers and antique tubs, and all have antique porcelain pedestal sinks and brass fixtures. The inn is just a five-minute walk from the center of town. *10 Lyon St., 02554, tel. 508/228–5040. 7 rooms. Air-conditioning. MC, V. Closed mid-Dec.–mid-Apr. CP. www.nantucket.net/lodging/lyonstreetinn*

**$$$–$$$$** **MANOR HOUSE.** The screened and open porches of this 1846 house in the heart of the historic district are perfect for a casual bit of people-watching. Rooms are spacious, with reproduction rice-carved beds (king or queen). Seven rooms have king canopy beds and working fireplaces. All rooms are no-smoking and have TV and phones. A small cottage next door done in wicker and chintz has two bedrooms and a fully equipped kitchen. Packages are available. *31 Centre St., Box 1436, 02554, tel. 508/228–0600 or 800/673–4559, fax 508/325–4046. Air-conditioning, concierge. 15 rooms, 1 cottage. D, MC, V. CP. www.oneweb.com/nantucket*

**$$$–$$$$** **TUCKERNUCK INN.** Home of the seasonal American Bounty (☞ Eating Out), just one block from the harbor, and about four blocks from Main Street, Tuckernuck has plenty of room in which to stretch out. You can choose from rather simply furnished and spacious rooms or two suites—all have a faint contemporary-country style, with braided rugs, quilts, ceiling fans, and phones with voice mail. You'll want to take in the view from the widow's walk, which surveys the town and harbor, and the secluded, sloping back lawn has space for all sorts of activities, like lawn chess. If you're coming in the off-season, you'll be treated to an expanded Continental breakfast November through late April. *60 Union St., 02554, tel. 508/228–4886 or 800/228–4886, fax 508/228–4890. 16 rooms, 2 suites. Restaurant, air-conditioning, in-room data ports, refrigerators, badminton, croquet, library. AE, MC, V. CP. www.tuckernuckinn.com*

**$$$–$$$$** ★ **UNION STREET INN.** With original wood paneling, pine floors, working fireplaces, and four-poster antique beds, this 1770 inn is best appreciated by those seeking a carefully restored Colonial atmosphere—although all rooms also have a cable TV. Lux duvets and robes inspire lounging about. It's close to Straight Wharf shops and ferries and the historic district. Unlike other island inns, Union Street prepares a full, home-cooked breakfast. You'll be served in the dining room or you can take it outside on the garden patio, shaded by tall trees. Children over five are welcome. *7 Union St., 02554, tel. 508/228–9222 or 800/225–5116, fax 508/325–0848. 14 rooms. Air-conditioning, concierge. AE, MC, V. BP. www.union-street-inn.com*

**$$$–$$$$** ★ **WESTMOOR INN.** Built in 1917 as a Vanderbilt summer house, this yellow Federal-style mansion with widow's walk and portico is a mile from town and a short walk to a quiet ocean beach, just off the Madaket bike path. There are plenty of places to settle down to read, including a wide lawn set with Adirondack chairs and a garden patio secluded behind 11-ft hedges. A wicker-filled sunroom has a common TV. Guest rooms are beautifully decorated in French-country style, most with soft florals and stenciled walls. One extra-large first-floor room has a giant bath with whirlpool tub and French doors opening onto the lawn. Some third-floor rooms are built into the eaves, which gives them charmingly odd angles and low ceilings—be sure to watch your head. During breakfast you can look out through the dining room's glass walls and ceiling. The inn is no-smoking. *Cliff Rd., 02554, tel. 508/228–0877 or 888/236–7310, fax 508/228–5763. 14 rooms. Bicycles. AE, MC, V. Closed early Dec.–mid-Apr. CP. www.westmoorinn.com*

**$$$–$$$$** **WOODBOX INN.** Built in 1709, the Woodbox lays claim to being Nantucket's oldest inn, and architectural details such as low, hand-hewn beams and wide floorboards mark it as a veritable antique. The rooms are somewhat small and appointed with antiques; three have queen-size beds, and six are suites with sitting rooms and one or two bedrooms. Some have working fireplaces. The highly acclaimed restaurant, the Woodbox (☞ Eating Out), serves breakfast and dinner and hosts special events, like wine tastings and weddings. *29 Fair St., 02554, tel. 508/228–1468. 3 rooms, 6 suites. Restaurant. No credit cards. Closed Dec.–June.*

**$$–$$$$ CENTURY HOUSE.** This 1833 late-Federal-style sea captain's home became a rooming house in the 1870s and has operated as a guest house ever since. Rooms are furnished with a mix of antiques and reproductions, but all the beds are beautiful old pieces—sleigh beds, spool beds, and canopy four-posters. The common room is filled with good books to read and has an eclectic, comfortable feel. A lavish buffet breakfast is served in the pine-panel country kitchen; if you're feeling languid, you can relax in a rocking chair on the wraparound veranda. The innkeepers also manage two cottages, one in 'Sconset across from the beach, another on Nantucket harbor. *10 Cliff Rd., 02554, tel. 508/228–0530; 561/655–3127 off-season. 14 rooms. MC, V. Closed mid-Oct.–mid-May. CP. www.centuryhouse.com*

**$$–$$$$ CHESTNUT HOUSE.** If you love fine crafts and friendly folks, stay at this charming, centrally located guest house, which is filled with hand-hooked rugs made by innkeeper Jerry Carl and paintings and baskets done by his wife and co-operator, Jeannette. There are also lovely Tiffany-style lamps created by their son. The guest parlor reflects the Arts and Crafts style, and some rooms have William Morris–theme wallpapers. Suites have a sitting room with sofa. A spacious, cheery cottage sleeps four (queen-size bed and sofa bed) and has a full kitchen and bath and a small deck. Rates include a voucher for breakfast at a couple of local restaurants. No smoking is permitted. *3 Chestnut St., 02554, tel. 508/228–0049, fax 508/228–9521. 1 room, 4 suites, 1 cottage. AE, MC, V. BP. www.chestnuthouse.com*

**$$–$$$$ THE GREY LADY.** Perched above an antiques shop and gallery in the historic district, the Grey Lady has cheerful rooms, some with private entrances. Innkeeper Rosalie Maloney, owner for 32 years—a long time in this business—actually welcomes pets, a rare island accommodation. All suites have TV and phone. Complimentary coffee is available in the sitting room, which also has a microwave and toaster for preparing your own snacks. The restored **Boat House Cottage**, also overseen by Maloney, on Old North Wharf ($550 daily, $4,000 weekly), overlooks the harbor and has heat, air-conditioning, a Franklin stove, laundry, and parking. *34 Centre St., Box 1292, 02554, tel. 508/228–9552 or 800/245–9552, fax 508/228–2115. 6 suites, 1 cottage. Air-conditioning, minibars. Closed Jan.–Apr. BP www.nantucket.net/lodging/greylady*

**$$–$$$$** **MARTIN HOUSE INN.** Debbie Wasil's friendly and very nicely refurbished B&B in an 1804 house offers a great variety of mostly spacious rooms (two suites and singles among them) with four-poster beds or canopies, pretty linens, and fresh flowers; several have queen-size beds, couches, and/or writing tables. Four rooms have fireplaces, including No. 21 on the second floor, which also has a queen-size canopy bed and a private porch overlooking the backyard. Third-floor shared-bath rooms are sunny and bright, with a quirky under-eaves feel. The large living room with a fireplace and the wide porch invite lingering. *61 Centre St., Box 743, 02554, tel. 508/228–0678, fax 508/325–4798. 11 rooms, 4 with shared bath; 2 suites. Piano. AE, MC, V. CP.*

**$$–$$$$** **ROBERTS HOUSE INN.** Roberts House is one of four attractive historical B&Bs in the thick of Nantucket's shops and restaurants co-owned by Sara and Michael O'Reilly—the others include the neighboring Manor House (☞ *above*), Periwinkle Guest House & Cottage, and the Linden House. From the Roberts Inn front porch at the corner of India and Centre streets, you can relax on the white-wicker furniture and read or people watch. Inside, the guest rooms are decorated with a mix of antique and reproduction furniture, including a poster or lace-canopy queen bed. Some rooms have high ceilings, fireplaces, and hot tubs. All have TV, phones, and small refrigerators. The bathrooms have a simple shower and complimentary toiletries. *11 India St., Box 1436, 02554, tel. 508/228–9009 or 800/872–6817, fax 508/325–*

*4046. 24 rooms. Air-conditioning, refrigerators, hot tubs. D, MC, V. CP. www.robertshouseinn.com*

**$$–$$$$ STUMBLE INNE.** On quiet Orange Street, a bit of a walk from town, this inn with the pun for a name is well worth the stroll. Each room is individually done, with antique furnishing, painted woodwork, soft colors, and Oriental rugs. Most have queen-size beds, private baths, TV, and phones. Breakfast is served in the dining room, and you can relax in the parlor, which is stocked with books and videos. Tucked privately away on the back lawn is the Garden Cottage, with two bedrooms, a fully equipped kitchen, living room, and deck. *109 Orange St., 02554, tel. 508/228–4482, fax 508/228–4752. 7 rooms, 1 cottage. Air-conditioning, refrigerators. AE, MC, V. CP. www.nantucket.net/lodging/stumbleinne*

**$$$ ★ ANCHOR INN.** In a quiet section of town but still close to shops and restaurants, Anchor Inn occupies a former private home built in 1806. Its sloping wide-plank floors, wainscoting, and period antiques help maintain its historical feel. The inn has rooms on three floors, with sweet names such as Wanderer and Morning Star. Most have queen-size, canopy beds, and all have TVs and phones with voice mail. A cozy enclosed porch serves as a breakfast room, an outside patio is great for lazy afternoons, and a comfortable common room is perfect for curling up with a book. Resident innkeepers Charles and Ann Balas, owners since 1983, are accommodating hosts, who serve delicious homemade muffins for breakfast. *66 Centre St., Box 387, 02554, tel. 508/228–0072. 11 rooms. Air-conditioning. AE, MC, V. Closed mid-Dec.–Feb. CP. www.anchor-inn.net*

**$$$ SAFE HARBOR.** Children and pets are welcome at this homey B&B with an enviable location just a stroll from Children's Beach. Most rooms have views of the harbor or town and are decorated with American and Oriental antiques. The West Wind and South Wind rooms are the largest; and South Wind and Zephyr have small private decks. Those without decks can relax on the wide front porch or sit on the quiet lawn, bordered by tall hedges. *2 Harborview Way, 02554, tel./fax 508/228–3222. 5 rooms. Fans. AE, MC, V. CP. www.beesknees.net/safeharbor*

**$$$ SEVEN SEA STREET.** You can get a lovely view of the harbor from this inn's widow's walk. There's a dash of Scandinavia inside, with plenty of tongue-in-groove light pine and red oak walls, some stenciled white walls, exposed-beam ceilings, and highly polished wide-board floors. Most rooms have braided rugs, queen-size beds with fishnet canopies and quilts, modern baths, and a desk area. All have TV/VCR, phones, and mini-refrigerators. The Honeymoon Suite, good for longer stays, has a cathedral post-and-beam ceiling, a full kitchen, a gas fireplace, and a view of the harbor. The inn is no smoking and is open year-round. *7 Sea St., 02554, tel. 508/228–3577, fax 508/228–3578. 11 rooms, 2 suites. Air-conditioning, mini-refrigerators, hot tub, steam room, library. AE, D, MC, V. CP. www.sevenseastreetinn.com*

**$$$ ★ SHIPS INN.** Located on quiet Fair Street, a bit above town, this historic inn was originally the home of whaling captain Obed Starbuck, and guest rooms are named for ships he commanded. Built in 1831, the inn was also the birthplace of abolitionist Lucretia Mott. Rooms are done with period antiques, pretty wallcovering, and flowers and have refrigerators, TVs, and phones. You'll have use of a spacious downstairs sitting room. The on-site eponymously named restaurant is acclaimed for the creative offerings of chef-owner Mark Gottwald, served in a romantic, candlelit setting. *13 Fair St., 02554, tel. 508/228–6524, fax 508/228–6524. 10 rooms, 2 with shared bath. Restaurant, air-conditioning. AE, MC, V. Closed Dec.–Apr. CP. www.nantucket.net/lodging/shipsinn*

**$$–$$$ CLIFF LODGE.** Owners Debby and John Bennett have preserved much of the old-house feeling of this 18th-century inn. Moldings, wainscoting, and wide-board floors hark back two centuries or so; the large rooms have pastel hooked rugs on spatter-painted floors, country curtains and furnishings, and down comforters.

Also in keeping with the house's age, some baths are quite small. The very pleasant apartment has a living room with a fireplace, a private deck and entrance, and a large eat-in kitchen. In addition to enjoying the attractive common rooms, you can lounge on the sunporch or garden patio, or head up to the roof walk for a great view of the harbor. Smoking is not permitted. *9 Cliff Rd., 02554, tel. 508/228–9480, fax 508/228–6308, 11 rooms, 1 apartment. MC, V. CP. www.nantucket.net/lodging/clifflodge*

**$$–$$$** ★ **18 GARDNER STREET.** The rooms in the 1835 house are comfortable without being completely casual, with wide-board floors, mostly queen-size beds (some canopy or four-poster) with eyelet sheets and handmade quilts, and a handful of antiques. Ten rooms have working fireplaces; all have TVs. The two-bedroom suite has two bathrooms and a living room. Another suite, with high ceilings, has a living room and a private entrance. Breakfast trays are available for taking your morning meal back to your room. Tea and homemade cookies are served in the afternoon. The inn is no smoking. *18 Gardner St., 02554, tel. 508/228–1155 or 800/435–1450, fax 508/325–0181. 17 rooms, 15 with bath; 2 suites. Air-conditioning, refrigerators, bicycles. AE, MC, V. CP. www.bandbnantucket.com*

**$$–$$$** **HAWTHORN HOUSE.** Innkeepers Mitch and Diane Carl have filled their 1850 house with art, hooked rugs, and stained glass. The smoke-free rooms are decorated with antiques and homey, personal touches, such as Mitch's stained-glass lamps and Diane's handmade quilts, and the upstairs common room is equally cozy. Another common room has a TV. A separate cottage sleeps two and has air-conditioning. Breakfast vouchers are included for three local restaurants. *2 Chestnut St., 02554, tel./fax 508/228–1468. 9 rooms, 7 with bath; 1 cottage. Fans, refrigerators. MC, V. BP. www.hawthorn-house.com*

**$$–$$$** **PINEAPPLE INN.** The pineapple was a symbol of hospitality in colonial times and such old traditions are alive and thriving in this

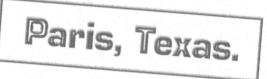

notable 1838 Greek Revival inn, once a whaling captain's home. Named after local whaling captains, the rooms have king or queen four-poster canopy beds with goose-down quilts, antiques, and spacious baths (with complementary Caswell-Massey toiletries) finished in white marble, as well as phones and voice mail. (The carefully refurbished rooms are not suited for children.) Innkeepers Caroline and Bob Taylor are former restaurant owners, so you'll have no cereal from a box here—instead morning diners are greeted with fresh-squeezed juices, espresso, and scrumptious homemade pastries. When the weather's warm, you can take your breakfast out to the brick garden patio. The inn is three blocks from the ferry landing on a small one-way street, and the owners will happily make suggestions for your stay. *10 Hussey St., 02554, tel. 508/228–9992, fax 508/325–6051. 12 rooms. Air-conditioning, in-room data ports. AE, MC, V. Closed mid-Dec.–Apr. CP. www.pineappleinn.com*

**$$–$$$** **76 MAIN STREET.** Built in 1883 by a sea captain, this no-smoking B&B just beyond the bustle of the shops carefully blends antiques and reproductions, Oriental rugs, handmade quilts, and lots of fine woodwork. The cherry-wood Victorian entrance hall is dominated by a long, elaborately carved staircase. Room No. 3, originally the dining room, also has wonderful woodwork, a carved-wood armoire, and twin four-poster beds. Spacious No. 1, once the front parlor, has three large windows, massive redwood pocket doors, and a bed with eyelet spread and canopy. The motel-like rooms in the 1955 annex out back, set around a flagstone patio and gardens, have low ceilings but are quite spacious and are perfect for families. Owner Shirley Peters usually officiates over breakfast, which she serves in the bright kitchen; her homemade scones are wonderful. *76 Main St., 02554, tel. 508/228–2533. 18 rooms. Refrigerators. AE, D, MC, V. Closed Jan.–Mar. CP. www.nantucketonline.com/lodging/76main*

**$–$$** ★ **NESBITT INN.** The innkeepers, Dolly Noblit (née Nesbit) and Nobby Noblit, are the third generation of Nesbitts to run this longstanding guest house since it was purchased by the family in 1914. Comfortable, shared-bath rooms are sweetly done in Victorian style, with lace curtains, some marble-top and brass antiques, and a sink. There's a pair of inexpensive single rooms, as well as a pair of rooms with two twin beds apiece. Some beds are not as firm as they should be, and the location next door to a popular bar-restaurant means it gets traffic noise (ask for a room on the quieter side), but the Nesbitt is a very good buy in this town. The backyard is perfect for children, and the owners couldn't be nicer. *21 Broad St., Box 1019, 02554, tel. 508/228–0156, fax 508/228–2446. 12 rooms without bath. No-smoking rooms, refrigerators. MC, V. Closed Jan.–Mar. CP.*

**$ STAR OF THE SEA YOUTH HOSTEL.** One of the most picturesque hostels in the country, this 49-bed Hostelling International facility occupies a former lifesaving station on Surfside Beach, a 3-mi ride from town on the bike path. The hostel has common areas, a piano, a kitchen, and grills for cookouts, as well as a variety of educational, cultural, and recreational programs. There are no private rooms and the doors lock at 11 PM, after which time you're on your own. Reservations, essential in July and August, are always strongly recommended, since the price is a low, low $15 a night. *31 Western Ave., 02554, tel. 508/228–0433 (Nov.–Mar.: Box 3158, West Tisbury 02575, tel. 508/693–2665 or 617/531–0459). Picnic area, volleyball, coin laundry. MC, V. Closed mid-Oct.–mid-Apr. www.hiayh.org/ushostel/nengreg/nantuc.htm*

## LODGING ELSEWHERE

**$$$$ SUMMER HOUSE.** Here, across from 'Sconset Beach and clustered around a flower-filled lawn, are the rose-covered cottages associated with Nantucket summers. Each one- or two-bedroom guest cottage is furnished in romantic, English-country style: trompe-l'oeil-bordered white walls, white eyelet spreads, and stripped English-pine antique furnishings. Some cottages have fireplaces or kitchens, and most have marble baths with whirlpool tubs. From the

Adirondack chairs on the lawn, read a book or just absorb the setting and the ocean view. The eponymously named restaurant (☞ Eating Out; reservations essential), also with ocean views, has superattentive service and live piano music. Daily seafood specials are often the menu highlights. The Ocean Restaurant serves lunch only. The pre–World War II whitewashed beach-cottage look lends the dining room a sort of *Great Gatsby* vibe. *17 Ocean Ave., Box 880, 'Sconset 02564, tel. 508/257–4577, fax 508/257–4590. 8 cottages. 2 restaurants, bar, piano bar, pool. AE, MC, V. Closed Nov.–late Apr. CP.*

**$$$$** ★ **WAUWINET.** This elegant, historic 19th-century hotel is the height of luxury on Nantucket, offering every amenity and service along with an exquisite location, impeccable furnishings, and a first-rate restaurant. On an unspoiled, removed corner of the island, the resort has a sweeping lawn with white chaise longues that leads to a pebbly private harbor beach, where you can play with a life-size wooden chess set. Guest rooms and cottages are individually decorated in country-beach style, with pine antiques; some have water views. Activities here include sailing, boat shuttles to Coatue beach, and, perhaps best of all, a Land Rover tour of the Great Point reserve—all of which are included in the room rate. Jitney service to and from Nantucket Town, 8 mi away, plus Steamship pickup, makes it convenient if you don't have a car. In season, you can cruise to the inn in the gorgeous *Wauwinet Lady* skiff. Topper's restaurant (☞ Eating Out) is tasteful and elegant (dinner reservations essential). *120 Wauwinet Rd., Box 2580, Nantucket 02584, tel. 508/228–0145 or 800/426–8718, fax 508/228–7135. 25 rooms, 5 cottages. Restaurant, bar, room service, 2 tennis courts, croquet, beach, boating, mountain bikes, library, concierge, business services. AE, DC, MC, V. Closed Nov.–Apr. BP. www.wauwinet.com*

**$$–$$$$** **WADE COTTAGES.** On a bluff overlooking the ocean, this complex of guest rooms, apartments, and cottages in 'Sconset couldn't be better located for those whose summer includes a lot of visits to the beach. The buildings, in the same family since the 1920s, are arranged around a central lawn with a great ocean view. Most

# island lodging

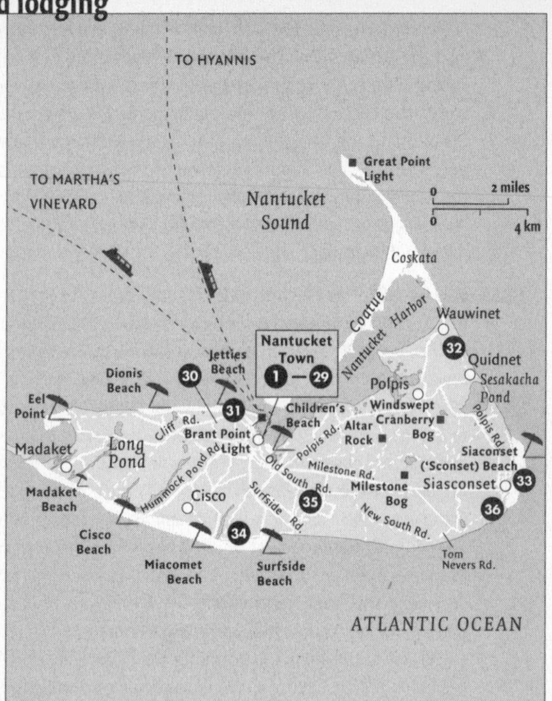


Cliffside Beach Club, 31

Nantucket Inn, 35

Star of the Sea Youth Hostel, 34

Summer House, 36

Wade Cottages, 33

Wauwinet, 32

Westmoor Inn, 30

inn rooms and cottages have sea views, and all have phones. Furnishings are generally in somewhat worn beach style, with some antique pieces. Note the minimum-stay requirements: three nights for rooms, one week for apartments, 2 weeks for cottages. Smoking is permitted. *Shell St., Box 211, 'Sconset 02564, tel. 508/257–6308; 212/989–6423 off-season; fax 508/257–4602. 8 rooms, 4 with bath; 6 apartments; 3 cottages. Refrigerators, badminton, Ping-Pong, beach, coin laundry. AE, MC, V. Closed mid-Oct.–late May. CP.*

**$$$ NANTUCKET INN.** Nantucket's only true hotel combines peace and quiet with convenience by offering hourly shuttle services into town, to the Steamship Authority dock, and to nearby Surfside Beach. Rooms are less generic than you might expect, many have high cathedral ceilings and decorative fireplaces and are arranged around landscaped grounds and courtyards. Mini-refrigerators, ironing boards, and TVs are provided in-room, and children are welcome. (Those under 18 stay free in their parents' room). There are also cottages available, one with a fireplace. The on-site Windsong restaurant (☞ Eating Out) serves breakfast and dinner and, every so often, a clambake. Package plans are available. *27 Macy's La., 3 mi from Nantucket Town, 02554, tel. 800/321–8484, 94 rooms, 6 cottages. Restaurant, bar, lounge, indoor pool, 2 tennis courts, health club, conference facilities, airport shuttle. AE, MC, V. Closed Dec.–Apr. www.nantucket.net/lodging/nantucketinn*

## REAL ESTATE AGENTS

If you're going to be staying for a week or more, you may want to consider renting a house, an arrangement that gives you a chance to settle in and get a real taste of island living. With your own kitchen, you won't have to eat out for every meal, and you can enjoy such homey summer pleasures as barbecues. Many find that staying in a house is more relaxing than a hotel or an inn, and much easier with children—even if you have to tow your own linens.

Finding a great rental house can be tough, however, especially since so many are often rented by the same folks year-to-year. Cast about your friends for a lead, but if nothing comes your way by word of mouth, you can turn to one of these local agents. Be forewarned, in summer, houses rent for about $10,000 a week, more for waterfront properties. In the off-season, prices drop to $5,000–$7,000. Discounts of 5% or so are standard if you rent for the whole season.

**Coffin Real Estate** (tel. 508/228–1138) is a reputable company with offices in town and in 'Sconset.

**Congdon & Coleman Real Estate** (tel. 508/325–5000), which has been around since 1931, handles a lot of house rentals.

**Denby Real Estate** (tel. 508/228–2522), associated with Sotheby's, specializes in waterfront rentals.

**Maury People** (tel. 508/228–1881), has some 1,500 private homes in its rental inventory including historic and beach homes.

# PRACTICAL INFORMATION

## Addresses

Some businesses have a street address *without* a number, especially if they're in an outlying area.

## Air Travel

### CARRIERS

Major carriers leave from New York area airports or Boston. American Eagle/American Airlines flies from Boston in season (May 26–September 11) and from New York (JFK) year-round. Continental Express flies from Newark, New Jersey, and Martha's Vineyard during the season. US Airways Express is operated by Colgan Air, and flies from Martha's Vineyard in season and from New York (LaGuardia) and Boston year-round.

The smaller carriers fly from Hyannis on Cape Cod year-round. Island Airlines has daily flights. Cape Air also flies from New Bedford, Martha's Vineyard, Boston, and Providence year-round. Island and Nantucket Airlines also have charters.

Prices on a large or small carrier are about the same. Charter flights are always more expensive.

➤ **MAJOR CARRIERS: American Eagle/American Airlines** (tel. 800/433–7300). **Continental Express** (tel. 800/525–0280). **US Airways Express** (tel. 800/428–4322).

➤ **SMALLER CARRIERS: Cape Air** (tel. 800/352–0714). **Island Airlines** (tel. 508/228–7575; 800/248–7779 in MA; 800/248–7779). **Nantucket Airlines** (tel. 508/228–6234 or 800/635–8787).

➤ **CHARTER CARRIERS: Air New England** (tel. 508/693–8899 or 800/693–8899). **Air Service, Inc.** (tel. 508/945–7458 or 800/872–1704). **Chatham Air Charter** (tel. 508/945–1976). **Desert & Island Air Charter, LLC** (tel. 800/835–9135). **Executive Jet Charter Services** (tel. 888/393–2853). **Ocean Wings** (tel. 508/325–5548,

508/228–3350, or 800/253–5039). **Westchester Air** (tel. 914/761–3000 or 800/759–2929).

### CHECK-IN & BOARDING

**Get to the gate and check in as early as possible,** especially during peak periods. Always **bring a government-issued photo ID to the airport.** You may be asked to show it before you are allowed to check in.

### FLYING TIMES

It's 50 minutes from Boston, one hour and 15 minutes from New York, 15 minutes from Hyannis and Martha's Vineyard, and 45 minutes from T. F. Green Airport in Providence.

## Airport

**Nantucket Memorial Airport** (tel. 508/325–5300) is about 3½ mi southeast of town via Old South Road. The terminal building is bright, modern, and comfortable, with ATM machines and rest rooms, and there's a restaurant and gift shop to occupy your time in case of delays. Some car rental agencies are based here. Taxi service to town costs $7, plus $1 for each additional person.

For pilots of private planes, the airport tower is controlled (between 0600 and 2100 in the summer) year-round, and there's an instrument-landing system on Runway 6-24 (6,303'). Overnight parking and tie-downs are available. Aircraft repair and servicing facilities are available on premises by calling Grey Lady Aviation.

➤ PRIVATE PLANE CONTACTS: **Grey Lady Aviation** (tel. 508/228–5888). **Nantucket Memorial Airport** (tel. 508/325–5307 operations; 508/325–5300 manager).

## Bike Travel

The main bike trails are paved, but mountain bikes (or street-and-mountain–bike hybrids) are best if you plan to explore the dirt roads; cobblestones on Main Street make for rough riding, too. There are several places to rent bicycles in town (☞

Outdoor Activities and Sports). Look for bike stands along Main Street, as there aren't many on side streets. **Obey all bike rules,** including signaling for turns, giving a clear warning when passing, and observing one-way roads. You must **walk your bike if you're going the wrong way** or you can be fined. Note that Massachusetts law requires children under 13 to wear protective helmets when they are operating a bike or riding as a passenger.

Bicycle paths are very clearly marked. Both the Chamber of Commerce and the visitor information bureau (☞ Visitor Information, *below*) have maps and free guides. Bike rental shops have maps, too.

## Boat & Ferry Travel

Hyannis ferries serve Nantucket year-round. Hy-Line has two boats, one of which runs between Nantucket and the Vineyard in summer only. The only way to get a car to Nantucket is on the Steamship Authority. To get a car from the Vineyard to Nantucket off-season, you have to return to Woods Hole, drive to Hyannis, and ferry it out from there.

### FARES & SCHEDULES

Hy-Line ferries based in Hyannis make three to five round-trips daily in high season (June to mid-September) and one daily round-trip in the last two weeks of May and September. On the high-speed year-round catamaran, there are five round-trips daily, six on Friday and in high season. Ferries for Oak Bluffs, on Martha's Vineyard, make three round-trips daily in season.

The Steamship Authority's Fast Ferry makes five daily round-trips from Hyannis late May to early January, six on Friday, weekends, and holidays. The regular ferry makes three round-trips in the off-season (late October to mid-May) and six round-trips in high season.

From Harwich Port, Freedom Cruise Line runs three daily round-trips in high season and one round-trip daily mid-May to mid-June and mid-September to mid-October.

## FROM HYANNIS

The Steamship Authority runs car-and-passenger ferries to Nantucket year-round. The trip takes 2¼ hours. If you plan to bring a car in summer or weekends in the fall, you *must* have a reservation. Book as far ahead as possible: Call weekdays from 5 AM to 9:55 PM. If you have a confirmed car reservation, be at the terminal 30 minutes (off season) or 45 minutes (in season) before sailing time. There are no standby reservations to Nantucket.

The Steamship Authority Fast Ferry Line runs from May 26 to January 3 and takes just an hour. Although reservations are not necessary, they're highly recommended.

Hy-Line's high-end, high-speed boat, the *Grey Lady II*, ferries passengers year-round. The trip takes just under an hour. That speed has its downside in rough seas—lots of bucking and rolling that some find nauseating. Seating ranges from benches on the upper deck to airlinelike seats in side rows of the cabin to café-style tables and chairs in the cabin front. There is a snack bar on board.

Hy-Line's slower ferry makes the 1¾- to 2-hour trip early May–October 28. In addition to basic service, the M.V. *Great Point* has a first-class section ($21 one-way) with a private lounge, rest rooms, upholstered seats, carpeting, complimentary Continental breakfast or afternoon cheese and crackers, a bar, and a snack bar.

➤ **HYANNIS FERRIES: Hy-Line High Speed** (*Grey Lady*: Ocean St. dock, tel. 508/778–0404 or 800/492–8082. Adults one-way $31, round-trip $55; children 13 mos.–age 12 one-way $25, round-trip $40; infants 12 mos. and under free; bicycles one-way $5). **Hy-Line ferry** (*Great Point*: Ocean St. dock, tel. 508/778–2602 reservations; 508/778–2600 information; 508/228–3949 on Nantucket. Adults one-way $12.50; children 5–12 one-way $6.25; bicycles one-way $5). **Steamship Authority** (South St. dock, tel. 508/477–8600; 508/228–3274 reservations; 508/228–0262 information; 508/540–1394 TTD. Passengers one-way $12.50, bicycles one-way $5. Cars one-way mid-May–mid-Oct. $158, mid-Oct.–mid-May $97). **Steamship Authority Fast Line** (South St. dock, tel. 508/495–3278 reservations. Adults one-way $23, round-trip $42; children 5–12 one-way $17.25, round-trip $31.50; children under 5 free; bicycles one-way $5, round-trip $10).

### FROM HARWICH PORT

Freedom Cruise Line runs passenger ferry service from May 15 to October 14 from Harwich Port west of Chatham on Cape Cod. The trip takes 90 minutes and offers an alternative to the Hyannis crowds. Reservations are highly recommended.

➤ HARWICH PORT FERRY: **Freedom Cruise Line** (Saquatucket Harbor, off Rte. 28, tel. 508/432–8999 reservations. Adults one-way $25, round-trip $39; children 2–12 one-way $20, round-trip $34; children under 2, $5 round-trip; bicycles one-way $5).

### FROM MARTHA'S VINEYARD

Hy-Line makes 2¼-hour runs to and from Nantucket from early June to mid-September—the only interisland passenger service.

➤ MARTHA'S VINEYARD FERRY: **Hy-Line** (tel. 508/778–2600 in Hyannis; 508/228–3949 on Nantucket; 508/693–0112 in Oak Bluffs. Adults one-way $12.50, round-trip $25; children 5–12 one-way $6.25, round-trip $12.50; bicycles one-way $5, round-trip $10).

### PRIVATE BOAT TRAVEL

Nantucket has first-class marina and mooring amenities for yacht and boat owners.

➤ MARINA CONTACTS: **Madaket Marine** (tel. 508/228–9086). **Nantucket Boat Basin** (tel. 508/228–1350 or 800/626–2628). **Nantucket Moorings** (tel. 508/228–4472). **Town Pier** (tel. 508/228–7260).

## Bus Travel

The Nantucket Regional Transit Authority runs shuttle buses in town and to Madaket, mid-island areas, 'Sconset, Surfside

Beach, and Jetties Beach. Service is usually from June 1 to September 30. Each of the five routes has its own schedule (you can pick one up at the Chamber of Commerce); service usually begins at 7 AM and ends at 11 PM. All shuttle buses have bike racks and lifts. Fares are 50¢ in town, $1 to 'Sconset and Madaket, $10 for a three-day pass, $15 for a seven-day pass, and $30 for a one-month pass. Seasonal passes are also available. Senior citizens over 65 and children under 6 ride free.

➤ **Shuttle Bus Contact: Nantucket Regional Transit Authority** (22 Federal St., Nantucket 02554, tel. 508/228–7025; 508/325–0788 TTY; www.nantucket.net/trans/nrta).

## Business Hours

Shops are generally open from 9 or 10 to 5, though in high season many downtown stores stay open until 10 PM or later. Except in Nantucket Town, shops are often closed on Sunday. For information on restaurants, *see* Eating Out.

Most historical sights and museums are open daily in summer and are closed or have very limited hours otherwise. Some events, such as corn grinding at the Old Mill or stargazing at Loines Observatory, are subject to weather conditions in summer.

## Car Rental

**Consider not using a car on Nantucket.** Having one is invariably expensive, and traffic and parking in town are just ghastly in season. Thus, you might find the experience of not having a car to bother with quite pleasant. If you're determined to rent a car during the high season **book early,** reserving such amenities as child/infant seats and bike racks. For a mid-size car with air-conditioning, you'll spend $90 per day or $550 per week in July, or $50 per day, $250 per week in the off-season. Jeep rentals are a whopping $175 per day, $995 per week in the summer, $90 per day or $450 per week in the off-season. To

drive on the beach or north of Wauwinet road to Coatue–Coskata–Great Point, you'll need an approved four-wheel-drive vehicle. Make sure your rental vehicle meets the park standards before you lay out your dough.

➤ MAJOR AGENCIES: **Budget** (tel. 508/228–5666, 888/228–5666). **Hertz** (tel. 508/228–9421, 800/654–3131). **Thrifty Car Rental** (tel. 508/325–4616, 800/367–2277).

➤ LOCAL AGENCIES: **Affordable Rentals** (tel. 508/228–3501 or 877/235–3500). **Around Nantucket Car Rentals** (tel. 508/228–5666 or 888/228–5666). **Nantucket Jeep Rental** (tel. 508/228–1618). **Nantucket Windmill** (tel. 508/228–1227 or 800/228–1227).

➤ NORTH-SHORE VEHICLE PERMITS: **Wauwinet Gatehouse** (end of Wauwinet Rd., tel. 508/228–0006).

## INSURANCE

When driving a rented car you are generally responsible for any damage to or loss of the vehicle as well as for any property damage or personal injury that you may cause. Before you rent see what coverage your personal auto-insurance policy and credit cards already provide. For about $15–$20 per day, rental companies sell protection, known as a collision- or loss-damage waiver (CDW or LDW), that eliminates your liability for damage to the car. **Make sure you have enough coverage to pay for the car.** If you do not have auto insurance or an umbrella policy that covers damage to third parties, purchasing liability insurance and a CDW or LDW is highly recommended.

## REQUIREMENTS & RESTRICTIONS

In Nantucket you must be 21 or older to rent a car, and rates may be higher if you're under 25. You'll pay extra for child seats (about $5 per day), which are compulsory for children under five, and for additional drivers (about $5 per day). Non-U.S. residents will need a reservation voucher, a passport, a driver's license, and a travel policy that covers each driver, when picking up a car.

### SURCHARGES

Unless it's absolutely necessary, don't plan to rent a car on Nantucket and take it off the island. **Consider renting a car in Hyannis,** where it may be much cheaper. Even if the agency allows it (which some don't), once you factor in the ferry charges you may as well have purchased a plane ticket. If you take the car off-island without the agency's permission and can't get it back on time, you may be subject to some very heavy fines. To avoid a hefty refueling fee, **fill the tank just before you turn in the car.** Some agencies charge an extra daily rate for additional drivers. **Don't try to circumvent additional driver charges** by changing drivers out of sight range of the agency. It's illegal for an unauthorized driver to operate a rental car, and if you are in an accident, all insurance (including your own) and waivers become null and void. You will be personally responsible for all damage and injuries.

## Car Travel

Whether you bring one over on the ferry or rent one when you arrive, driving a car here is a costly nuisance, especially in the summer. Do what you can to do without a car on Nantucket—you may be only really able to relax without it.

### GAS STATIONS

Due to freight costs, gas is pricey on-island. Expect to pay more than $2 per gallon and as much as $2.33 per gallon if your car has expensive tastes. Except for the airport gas station, all stations are mid-island. That is, there are no gas stations in town.

➤ GAS STATION LOCATIONS: **Airport Gas Station** (Macy's La., tel. 508/228–1742). **D&B Auto** (43 Sparks Ave., tel. 508/228–1571). **Hatch's Package Store** (129 Orange St., tel. 508/228–0131). **On-Island Gas** (34 Sparks Ave., tel. 508/228–7099).

### PARKING

During high season, parking in town is practically nonexistent. Park-and-ride locations are plentiful on the island. The Nantucket Regional Transit Authority (☞ Bus Travel, *above*) can supply information on locations and connecting shuttle schedules.

### RULES OF THE ROAD

Be alert for Nantucket's numerous one-way streets, "no left turn" intersections, and blocks closed to car traffic. Keep vehicles (and bikes for that matter) on roads and paths.

State law requires that you always **strap children who are 5 years old or younger or weigh 40 pounds or less into approved child-safety seats that are properly secured and installed.** Children who are 12 and under must wear seat belts regardless of where they're seated.

## Children in Nantucket

There's plenty to do for vacationing families here, from trips to the beach and minigolf to child-specific art classes and museum programs. Children's Beach hosts children's concerts, numerous camps, tie-dying workshops, and a theater program for young actors. There's also an evening camp for youngsters ages 5 to 13, from 6 PM to 9 PM, June through September at Murray Camp. It's a great opportunity for parents to get in a little alone time, while the children have a blast. Remember to **arrange for cribs, children's beds, and other such amenities** when you book your room or house rental.

➤ **CONTACTS:** Murray Camp of Nantucket (tel. 508/325–4600).

### BABYSITTING

Nantucket Babysitters' Service has year-round professional baby-sitting and home-helper services. The Peanut Gallery, a children's store on India Street (off Centre Street), often has informal postings.

➤ **BABY-SITTING CONTACTS: Nantucket Babysitters' Service** (tel. 508/228–4970).

## Emergencies

➤ **CONTACTS: Police or fire** (911). **Nantucket Cottage Hospital** (57 Prospect St., tel. 508/228–1200), a 24-hour medical and dental emergency room.

## Gay & Lesbian Travelers

Although Provincetown on the Cape is a popular destination for gays and lesbians, Nantucket is equally welcoming for those out and about.

➤ **GAY- & LESBIAN-FRIENDLY TRAVEL AGENCIES: Different Roads Travel** (8383 Wilshire Blvd., Suite 902, Beverly Hills, CA 90211, tel. 323/651–5557 or 800/429–8747, fax 323/651–3678). **Kennedy Travel** (314 Jericho Turnpike, Floral Park, NY 11001, tel. 516/352–4888 or 800/237–7433, fax 516/354–8849, www.kennedytravel.com). **Now Voyager** (4406 18th St., San Francisco, CA 94114, tel. 415/626–1169 or 800/255–6951, fax 415/626–8626, www.nowvoyager.com). **Skylink Travel and Tour** (1006 Mendocino Ave., Santa Rosa, CA 95401, tel. 707/546–9888 or 800/225–5759, fax 707/546–9891, www.skylinktravel.com), serving lesbian travelers.

## Health

A troublesome problem on Nantucket is Lyme disease. This bacterial infection is transmitted by deer ticks and can be very serious, leading to chronic arthritis and worse if left untreated. Pregnant women are advised to **avoid areas of possible deer tick infestation.** Deer ticks are most prevalent April–October but can be found year-round. They are about the size of a pinhead. Anyone planning to explore wooded areas or places with tall grasses (including dunes) should **wear long pants, socks drawn up over pant cuffs, and a long-sleeve shirt with a close-fitting**

**collar**; boots are also recommended. The National Centers for Disease Control recommends that DEET repellent be applied to skin (not face!) and that permethrin be applied to clothing directly before entering infested areas; **use repellents very carefully** and conservatively with small children. Ticks also attach themselves to pets. Also ask your physician about Lymerix, the new Lyme disease vaccine; it takes three shots and 12 months to be 80% effective. Always closely **check yourself within 12 hours** of nature excursions for any ticks you might have attracted.

If you wander into the woods or stray off a bike path, **be on the lookout for poison ivy,** a pervasive vinelike plant, recognizable by its leaf pattern: three shiny green leaves together. In spring, new poison-ivy leaves are red; likewise, they can take on a reddish tint as fall approaches. The oil from these leaves produces an itchy skin rash that spreads with scratching. If you think you may have touched some leaves, **wash as soon as you can** with soap and cool water.

Although the public beaches usually have lifeguards on duty throughout the summer, **beware of heavy undertows,** especially before or after a storm. Surfside Beach can be especially dangerous.

**Don't rent or drive a moped.** Even if you've experience with such things, the cobblestone streets in town are not at all conducive to smooth riding, and there are many distractions on the road. Accidents, many of them serious, are all too common.

## Lodging

Because the island has a large number of repeat visitors, Nantucket is the kind of place where often there's little to no vacancy for months at a time. **Make your lodging arrangements far in advance.** If you're on the island and stuck, the Nantucket Information Bureau (☞ Visitor Information, *below*) maintains a list of room availability in season and at holidays for last-minute bookings. At night, check the lighted board outside for available rooms.

If you're planning to stay at a bed-and-breakfast, be sure to **check in advance with the owners** to be sure that the B&B welcomes children. Some establishments are filled with fragile antiques, and owners may not accept children of a certain age.

Assume that hotels operate on the **European Plan** (EP, with no meals) unless we specify that they use the **Continental Plan** (CP, with a Continental breakfast), **Breakfast Plan** (BP, with a full breakfast), **Modified American Plan** (MAP, with breakfast and dinner), or the **Full American Plan** (FAP, with all meals).

### B&B RESERVATION AGENCIES

Most of these agencies can do more than find you a great B&B: many can also arrange any and all details of your visit.

➤ **B&B CONTACTS: DestINNations** (tel. 800/333–4667). **Heaven Can Wait Accommodations** (Box 622, Siasconset 02564, tel. 508/257–4000). **Martha's Vineyard and Nantucket Reservations** (Box 1322, 73 Lagoon Pond Rd., Vineyard Haven, Martha's Vineyard 02568, tel. 508/693–7200, 800/649–5671 in MA).

### HOUSE RENTALS

Many rent a house or cottage for a week or longer rather than stay at a B&B or hotel. A number of realtors (complete lists are provided by the Chamber of Commerce and the Nantucket Information Bureau; ☞ Visitor Information, *below*) have rentals ranging from in-town apartments in lovely old buildings to new waterfront houses (☞ Real Estate Agents in Where to Stay).

## Money Matters

Nantucket is expensive, plain and simple, but there are things you can do to cut costs—riding a bike around the island as well as eating simply at lunch counters and at your rental house can help. Free outdoor concerts and art galleries are also at your disposal, as are the beaches and wildlife areas. As for sightseeing, you can **purchase memberships or all-inclusive passes to Nantucket's historical sites.** Individual admissions vary, but you'll save money with all-inclusive passes for the Nantucket Historical Association (NHA) sites ($10 for adults, $5 for children 5 to 14) or the Maria Mitchell Association (MMA) sites ($7 for adults, $5 for senior citizens and children ages 6 to 14). With a few exceptions, prices throughout this guide are given for adults. Reduced fees are often available for children, students, and senior citizens.

### ATMS

➤ **ATM LOCATIONS: A&P** (Salem St., at Straight Wharf). **Fleet Bank** (24 hrs.: Pacific Club, Main and Federal Sts.). **Nantucket Bank** (2 Orange St., 104 Pleasant St., and Nantucket Memorial Airport; tel. 508/228–0580). **Pacific National Bank** (61 Main St.).

### CREDIT CARDS

Throughout this guide, the following abbreviations are used: **AE,** American Express; **D,** Discover; **DC,** Diners Club; **MC,** Master Card; and **V,** Visa.

➤ **REPORTING LOST CARDS:** To report lost or stolen credit cards, call the following toll-free numbers: **American Express** (tel. 800/ 327–2177). **Discover Card** (tel. 800/347–2683). **Diners Club** (tel. 800/234–6377). **MasterCard** (tel. 800/307–7309). **Visa** (tel. 800/ 847–2911).

## Packing

There's an old adage that goes something like, "Pack more money and fewer clothes than you think you'll need." This is doubly true on Nantucket. Unless you're bringing a car over, you'll either be toting your own bags on and off the ferry or squeezing them onto small planes with very limited luggage room. In short, pack light. Just a few restaurants require formal dress, as do some dinner cruises, but otherwise the area prides itself on informality. Do **pack a sweater or jacket, even in**

**summer,** as nights can be cool. Perhaps most important of all, **don't forget a swimsuit** (or two).

In your carry-on luggage, **pack an extra pair of eyeglasses or contact lenses** and **enough of any medication you take** to last the entire trip. You may also ask your doctor to write a spare prescription using the drug's generic name, since brand names may vary.

### CHECKING LUGGAGE

If you plan on bringing your bike, **ask when making reservations if the plane can accommodate your bike.** How many carry-on bags you can bring with you is up to the airline. Most allow two, but not always, so make sure that everything you carry aboard will fit under your seat or in the overhead bin, and get to the gate early.

## Sales Tax

Massachusetts state sales tax is 5%.

## Taxi

Taxis usually wait outside the airport or at the foot of Main Street by the ferry. Rates are flat fees, based on one person with two bags before 1 AM: $5 within town (1½-mi radius), $7 to the airport, $11 to 'Sconset, $13 to Wauwinet.

➤ TAXI SERVICE: **A-1 Taxi** (tel. 508/228–3330 or 508/228–4084). **Aardvark and Lisa's Cab** (tel. 508/228–2223). **All Point Taxi** (tel. 508/228–5779). **Betty's Tour & Taxi Service** (tel. 508/228–5786). **B. G.'s Taxi** (tel. 508/228–4146).

## Travel Agencies

A good travel agent puts your needs first. Look for an agency that has been in business at least five years, emphasizes customer service, and has someone on staff who specializes in your destination. In addition, **make sure the agency belongs to a professional trade organization.** The American Society of

Travel Agents (ASTA), with 27,000 agents in some 170 countries, is the largest and most influential in the field. Operating under the motto "Integrity in Travel," it maintains and enforces a strict code of ethics and will step in to help mediate any agent-client disputes if necessary. ASTA also maintains a Web site that includes a directory of agents.

➤ LOCAL AGENT REFERRALS: **American Society of Travel Agents** (ASTA; tel. 800/965–2782 24-hr hot line; fax 703/684–8319; www.astanet.com). **Association of British Travel Agents** (68–71 Newman St., London W1P 4AH, tel. 0171/637–2444, fax 0171/637–0713, www.abtanet.com). **Association of Canadian Travel Agents** (1729 Bank St., Suite 201, Ottawa, Ontario K1V 7Z5, tel. 613/237–3657, fax 613/521–0805). **Australian Federation of Travel Agents** (Level 3, 309 Pitt St., Sydney 2000, tel. 02/9264–3299, fax 02/9264–1085, www.afta.com.au). **Travel Agents' Association of New Zealand** (Box 1888, Wellington 10033, tel. 04/499–0104, fax 04/499–0827).

## Visitor Information

➤ VISITOR INFORMATION CONTACTS: **Chamber of Commerce** (48 Main St., 02554, tel. 508/228–1700). **Nantucket Visitor Services and Information Bureau** (25 Federal St., 02554, tel. 508/228–0925).

## Web Sites

Do check out the World Wide Web when you're planning your trip. You'll find everything from current weather forecasts to virtual tours of famous cities. Fodor's Web site, www.fodors.com, is a great place to start your online travels.

For general information and lodging resources, visit www.nantucketchamber.org, www.nantucket.net, or www.massvacation.com. Island ferry information and schedules are available from www.hy-linecruises.com (Hy-Line ferry service) and www.islandferry.com (Steamship Authority ferry service). For on-island transportation information, visit www.nantucket.net/trans/nrta (Nantucket Regional Transit Authority) or www.massbike.org (Massachusetts Bicycle Coalition). For information on accessibility in Massachusetts see www.state.ma.us/dem/access.htm (Directory of Accessible Facilities) or www.capecod.net/ccdad/ (Cape Cod Disability Access Directory).

## When to Go

Memorial Day through Labor Day (in some cases Columbus Day) is high season. This is summer with a capital S, a time for barbecues, beach bumming, water sports, and swimming. During summer everything is open for business, but you can also expect high-season evils: high prices, crowds, and traffic.

Nantucket is, however, becoming a year-round destination. Many shops and restaurants remain open through Nantucket Noel (Thanksgiving through December 31).

### CLIMATE

Although there are plenty of idyllic beach days, rain or fog is not an uncommon part of even an August vacation. Those who do not learn to appreciate the beauty of the land and sea in mist and rain may find themselves mighty cranky.

Temperatures in winter and summer are milder here than on the mainland, due in part to the warming influence of the Gulf Stream and the moderating ocean breezes. As a rule (and there have been dramatically anomalous years—1994 and 1999 in particular), the island gets much less snow than the mainland, and what falls generally does not last. Still, winter can bring bone-chilling dampness.

The following are average daily maximum and minimum temperatures for Nantucket.

➤ **FORECASTS:** For local Cape weather, coastal marine forecasts, and today's tides, call the weather line of **WQRC** in Hyannis (tel. 508/771–5522). **Weather Channel Connection** (tel. 900/932–8437), 95¢ per minute from a Touch-Tone phone.

## CLIMATE

| | | | | | | | | |
|---|---|---|---|---|---|---|---|---|
| **Jan.** | 40F | + 4C | **May** | 62F | 17C | **Sept.** | 70F | 21C |
| | 25 | − 4 | | 48 | +9 | | 56 | 13 |
| **Feb.** | 41F | + 5C | **June** | 71F | 22C | **Oct.** | 59F | 15C |
| | 26 | − 3 | | 56 | 13 | | 47 | 8 |
| **Mar.** | 42F | + 6C | **July** | 78F | 25C | **Nov.** | 48F | 9C |
| | 28 | − 2 | | 63 | 17 | | 37 | 3 |
| **Apr.** | 53F | 12C | **Aug.** | 76F | 24C | **Dec.** | 40F | 4C |
| | 40 | + 4 | | 61 | 16 | | 26 | −3 |

# INDEX

## S



## T



## U



## V



## W

## FODOR'S POCKET NANTUCKET

**EDITOR:** Melisse J. Gelula

**EDITORIAL CONTRIBUTORS:** Elizabeth Gehrman, Lynda Hammes, Sandy MacDonald, Bill Maple, Debi Stetson, Joyce Wagner

**EDITORIAL PRODUCTION:** Ira-Neil Dittersdorf

**MAPS:** David Lindroth, *cartographer*; Bob Blake and Rebecca Baer, *map editors*

**DESIGN:** Fabrizio La Rocca, *creative director*; Tigist Getachew, *art director*; Melanie Marin, *photo editor*

**PRODUCTION/MANUFACTURING:** Angela L. McLean

**COVER PHOTOGRAPH:** Catherine Karnow/Corbis

## COPYRIGHT



ISBN 0-679-00782-2

ISSN 1533-340X

## IMPORTANT TIP

Although all prices, opening times, and other details in this book are based on information supplied to us at press time, changes occur all the time in the travel world, and Fodor's cannot accept responsibility for facts that become outdated or for inadvertent errors or omissions. So **always confirm information when it matters,** especially if you're making a detour to visit a specific place.

## SPECIAL SALES

Fodor's Travel Publications are available at special discounts for bulk purchases for sales promotions or premiums. Special editions, including personalized covers, excerpts of existing guides, and corporate imprints, can be created in large quantities for special needs. For more information, contact your local bookseller or write to Special Markets, Fodor's Travel Publications, 280 Park Avenue, New York, NY 10017. Inquiries from Canada should be directed to your local Canadian bookseller or sent to Random House of Canada, Ltd., Marketing Department, 2775 Matheson Boulevard East, Mississauga, Ontario L4W 4P7. Inquiries from the United Kingdom should be sent to Fodor's Travel Publications, 20 Vauxhall Bridge Road, London SW1V 2SA, England.

PRINTED IN THE UNITED STATES OF AMERICA

10 9 8 7 6 5 4 3 2 1